Everyday Language
& Everyday Life

Everyday
Language
&
Everyday
Life

Richard Hoggart

Transaction Publishers
New Brunswick (U.S.A.) and London (U.K.)

Library of Congress Catalog Number: 2002075517
ISBN: 0-7658-0176-0
Printed in Canada

Library of Congress Cataloging-in-Publication Data

Hoggart, Richard, 1918-
    Everyday language and everyday life / Richard Hoggart.
        p. cm.
    Includes index.
    ISBN 0-7658-0176-0 (acid-free paper)
        1. English language—Spoken English—England. 2. Aphorisms and apothegms—History and criticism. 3. English language—Social aspects—England. 4. Proverbs, English—History and criticism. 5. English language—Variation—England. 6. English langauge—England—Idioms. 7. English language—England—Usage. 8. Working class—England—Language. 9. Speech and social status—England. 10. England—Social life and customs. 11. Maxims—History and criticism. 12. Figures of speech. I. Title.

PE1074.8 .H64 2003
306.44'0942—dc21

2002075517

In loving memory
of our sister, Molly

For last year's words belong to last year's language
And next year's words await another voice.

Contents

Acknowledgments

The works of most of the authors quoted here are out of copyright.

The few quotations from more modern authors are so small as to fall well within normally accepted limits for this kind of book. I am, of course, glad to acknowledge those authors (or executors) and publishers: Alan Bennett and the BBC, Jonathan Coe and Viking, the Executors of T. S. Eliot's Estate and Faber and Faber, Tony Harrison and Penguin, the Executors of Nancy Mitford's Estate and Hamish Hamilton, the Executors of George Orwell's Estate and Gollancz, and Alan Watkins and Duckworth.

As so often, I owe a great debt to Geoffrey Goodman, Stephen Hearst, and John Miller, all of them gifted readers and critics; and to Stephen Jones, without whom there would have been near chaos.

My warmest thanks are due also to Irving Louis Horowitz and Mary Curtis and all at Transaction Publishers for unstinting support over many years.

Last and as always, but no less deeply meant for that, my love and thanks to all the family and, in particular, to my wife Mary.

Preface

About a year ago, whilst looking rather casually through the preface to an earlier book, *A Measured Life* (1994), I came upon this sentence: 'You could write a book about the English character, warts and all, simply by putting together in thematic groups the traditional cant expressions that lubricate our daily life'.

I had entirely forgotten the idea, and did not even remember it throughout the year in which the present book was being written. Obviously, it had been lying dormant somewhere at the back of the mind. During that year, one part of the suggestion proved ill-judged: such a task is not at all a 'simple putting together'. It may begin in that way but it soon branches into its own complexities.

One thing was clear from the start. Such a book would best begin with the daily, conventional speech habits of a particular people in time and place, not with a scouring of dictionaries and linguistic records. If the examination of idioms, as they were habitually used, was to be revealing it should be rooted in a known, felt life. For me, that had to be the daily life of the Northern English working class from the 1930s onwards. So that was where I began; but did not remain.

I soon recovered from memory about one hundred and fifty common sayings of that period and class. But many, it was plain to see, were used also by people of other classes. Was there being illustrated here an aspect of the unity of English culture, a unity we sometimes claim, readily and with a certain pride, as strong and enduring?

That thought had some validity, but on further examination, not much. My class-of-birth used some sayings almost uniquely. More important, whilst they used some sayings they shared with other groups, they used certain of them more often and with greater stress than those other groups. Such sayings spoke most directly to them. Repetition and emphasis became defining characteristics.

A simple example: other groups occasionally used cant expressions about the experience of being 'hard up', on their 'beam-ends';

Originally, the Preface was intended for the American edition. However, Transaction, through its distributor in the United Kingdom—Eurospan—is publishing this original work on a worldwide basis in English.

they did not use them as often and with as much force as working-class people. It would have been odd, against experience, if they had. And so, my first substantially descriptive chapter is about 'poverty and its languages' as I had directly experienced them.

Then the broadening began. This being England, very many of those favourite sayings were rooted in the sense of class. But that is a portmanteau expression. Opened, it contains something of your assumed place in society, where you are and usually expect to remain in the pecking order—as defined by birth, education, occupation, even geography. It helps to form your sense of yourself, of your status as felt on the pulses.

At this point it seems to me that this book, which must at first sight be thought to be about things foreign to American readers, though perhaps interesting—as Lionel Trilling, in particular, found the jungle of English class habits—it might, in fact, be extremely relevant to their own world. That is why I used the word 'status' at the end of the preceding paragraph, in the conviction that the sense of status plays in American life something of the part played historically by the sense of class in England.

If that is so, then the role(s) played by conventional phrases may be powerful in the USA, as in England. But an American writer setting out to examine that hunch will first have the job of ground-clearing, which has hardly affected me.

As a society that publicly insists so much on its egalitarianism, America has produced a thicket of habits, phrases, styles of greeting, all of which are meant to insist on that, on the classless nature of U.S. society. There is some truth in the powerful assertions, but Americans, especially those eating low down on the hog, know their limits. An American writer will have to cut through that thicket carefully and surgically if the complex meanings of American conventional expressions at all levels are to be explored.

For studies in either nation, the next step, upon which I touch only slightly towards the end of this book, is to examine the ways in which new linguistic practices are beginning to replace the old linguistic worlds. Key elements in the persuasive mass media world are 'sound bites' and their short successive lives, and many other related offerings. Their socio-psychological role is insistently to offer all their 'consumers' a new sense of 'togetherness' within their society, and a new sense of their happy roles within it.

Richard Hoggart

Introduction

The origins and nature of this book are explained more fully in the first chapter. It emerged from my suddenly realising to how great an extent most everyday speech moves not by whole sentences but by a hopping from one ready-made phrase to another.

If one examined the phrases—epigrams, apophthegms and the like—most used by any single class of people at any one period, would the patterns reveal how, and how differently, distinct groups saw their lives?

I decided to look in this way at the favourite maxims of working-class people, as they were to be heard in Leeds during the twenties and thirties. Inevitably, the canvas broadened. For example, many of the expressions are still used by people whose parents and grandparents were indisputably working-class, but who might not identify themselves in that way today. Many such phrases were and still are used in other classes. But emphases may differ. So the field spreads outwards.

I put down from memory the bulk of those sayings. I refreshed memory by looking at various books of reference; and, as is always the case when you are pursuing a theme, more items kept coming into view by chance, from casual conversations as well as from general reading. The test for entry was that, if any item came to the surface by whatever means, I then realised that it had all the time been somewhere in my memory, chiefly from the prewar years. Once tapped, the reclaiming of such items was like the action of a trawl-net in the deep sea of memory.

I have used inverted commas around most of the phrases, but sometimes the narrative flowed better without them, so they were incorporated without the commas. Similarly, I have used demotic rather than 'educated' language when that seemed fitting; and used also some local as well as public forms.

Even the most tired writing, full of cliches, may serve a purpose at some time in our lives; as stepping stones. When the Fourth Form in my grammar school was taken for a week's camping at Stratford on Avon, to see several of Shakespeare's plays, I was asked to write a report on the visit for the school magazine. I looked at it again some time ago. It was crammed with what then seemed fine writers' phrases. They were in fact banal images and locutions picked up from the local newspaper and the popular magazines which occasionally came into our bookless house.

They had been adopted because I was becoming mildly drunk with language, like a boy on shandy; or like someone still unable to distinguish between cheap booze and fine wine. I could write neither plain, nor complex, English. Later, Samuel Butler and George Orwell helped me to some extent towards acquiring the first.

In more than one book I have included anecdotes about my own earlier life, especially in Hunslet. Given the nature of this book it was unavoidable that a few of them, especially those which illustrate the local use of language, should be repeated here. If this irritates any readers, I am sorry.

Apart from a brief introduction to the role of the mass media in a mass society, this may be my last book. It is certainly the last to be largely centred on the Northern English working class. Enough is enough.

1

Beginnings

How can I tell what I think till I see what I say?
—E. M. Forster (attributed)

Approaches

I belatedly realise that, if only half-consciously, I have been reg-
istering for years the oddity of one common speech habit. That is:
the fondness for employing ready-made sayings and phrasings whenever we open our mouths; a disinclination to form our own sentences 'from scratch', unless that becomes inescapable.

How far do the British, but particularly the English, share the same
sayings right across the social classes; and if each group uses some
different ones (though, on a first look, probably not many), are those
differences decided by location, age, occupation and place in the
social scale? Within each group, what decides which forms of conventional speech are most used and with what, if any, different degrees of emphasis?

The next step was to enquire whether, by looking at a particular
group's phrasings, one might understand better how its members
saw or simply responded to the most important elements in their
lives. Did such sayings, taken together, indicate some of the main
lines of their culture, its basic conditions, its stresses and strains, its
indications of meaning, of significance, and so on.

To do that for a whole society would be an enormous undertak-
ing, would mean sifting and 'better sifting' (to adopt a popular working-class formulation) through hundreds of sayings until, one might
hope, the shape of a particular but very complex and varied set of
overlapping cultures emerged. That could be a lifetime's work even
if one restricted it to a small country such as England. But 'small'
there obviously gives a false perspective. Though small in size, En-

1

gland manifestly has a long and rich history, and its language reflects that. Best—essential, for an amateur without access to elaborate computers—to narrow the focus. In my case, to focus on the
Northern English working class of my childhood.

My memory is still full of their patterns of speech; some I still use
day-by-day. How did we characteristically talk to each other in
Hunslet, Leeds, and what did our talk tell about the ways we responded to our common experiences? What psychological shape
did it all make; what did it reveal about our hopes and fears and our
responses to them? I expect to stray widely on the way; especially
into the war years and after; and will, as the material prompts, move
across different social classes.

But that was how this book began, by looking at the prewar Northern working class; and that is also why the next chapter, the first of
single-minded substance, is about being poor at that time and place.
Behind that and other chapters, all the time, is the question of how
much of that habitual speech survives into the very different circumstances of today; and what those sayings which are retained and
those newly minted tell us. Towards the end that matter of the newly
minted will be broached, but only lightly.

In *A Short Walk Down Fleet Street,* Alan Watkins has a nice observation on what has elsewhere been called 'breeze-block speech',
by which we put our conversation together as a series of loosely
linked, immediately-to-hand chunks: 'Real writers write in words;
most literate people in recognisable blocks of words; and politicians, commonly, in whole prefabricated sentences or sometimes
paragraphs'.

Most of us fall into a sub-division of the third group, into a simpler and less self-conscious version, as befits those who are not politicians or other kinds of public figures. Our speech is like a verbal
equivalent of those snakes that children make with dominoes on a
table, or interlocking parts in a very long but thin jig-saw, or a kind
of continuous-prefabricated-strip of sticky verbal labels. Many of us
rarely utter a sentence which has an individually chosen subject,
object and verb; or includes one simple adjective to indicate a quality or characteristic; nor would we often venture on a free, self-cho-
sen adverb. We move by jumping as if over a very tricky stream
from handy metaphor or image to handy borrowed phrase; spoken
hopscotch. It is both time- and worry-saving, and usually livelier, to
say: 'It's like finding a needle in a haystack'; or: 'They're leaving in

droves'; or 'That's just the tip of the iceberg', rather than putting together the necessary syntactical, non-metaphorical, bits and pieces.

All this is most helpful at grave or embarrassing moments, when we wish to skirt round a naked harsh truth. We would prefer not to say, straight: 'He is very old indeed and not likely to see the year out', since that can leave us feeling slightly rude and crude. We take refuge in a range of euphemisms, such as 'He can't be very long for this world'. That is only marginally softer than the more direct form, but it serves. It serves better than the blunt: 'He's on his last legs'. You would not use that in talking to one of his relatives; you might in the streets.

Evasion is naturally demanded at the death-bed. Auden deliberately avoided it. He used to tell how he went into the room where his father was dying and said: 'You know you are dying, father'. That would have been thought cruel in our district. It may be that Auden, as a devout and direct Christian, went on to suggest a proper Christian way for his father to pass his last hours; that that was more important to him than equivocation.

In other circumstances we may not be wholly evading. We may be merely lazy; or wish not too obviously to be 'laying it on the line'; or, conversely, may prefer to use an image sharper than our own speech to do our work for us. We are greatly 'taken by' alliterative couplings: 'fish, flesh, fowl or good red herring', 'hale and hearty', 'kith and kin', 'safe and sound'.

We do not say directly: 'She is a very proud woman' but 'She's as proud as a peacock'; that is usually simple laziness, almost a tic, taking the bit from the box. We avoid saying; 'He is a greedy child', which is hard to utter politely; oddly, we may prefer 'His eyes are bigger than his belly'; which strengthens the accusation, but can be safely invoked as a piece of acceptable, as much indulgent as rude, folk-language. Of a mean man the choice might well be: 'He wouldn't even give you the skin off his rice pudding'; which is pictorially witty; the homely comic touch slightly leavens the unavoidable harshness of a straightforward 'mean'. We hesitate to say flatly: 'He's a crook', even though he clearly is; instead, we say, 'He'd rob you as soon as look at you', which is both witty and cogent.

It is easy to identify evasion and laziness. Less common is that search for jokiness and colour, which are almost always borrowed from unknown wordsmiths. Old or new, all have to have at least one kind of attraction. The best are neat beyond all substitution. 'Wise after the event' would not be easy to replace economically and memorably.

So we jump from verbal stepping-stone to verbal stepping-stone over the deep and murky waters of the linguistic sea. We try to escape the need for a logically expressed succession in our speech; for that we hardly ever feel ready. We prefer the instantly available and comprehensible image. Recently, an executive on the radio spoke of someone or some idea which 'beat a path to my door' instead of saying, for instance, 'he/it could not be ignored'. Emerson's phrase, about the resulting stream of visitors to a man who has made a better mousetrap (Elbert Hubbard also claimed authorship) is much more vividly memorable. It is unlikely that more than one in a hundred who still makes use of it knows where the fancy came from. The same is true of Dr. Johnson's observation on a man's reaction to the prospect of hanging: 'it concentrates his mind wonderfully'.

Current and very frequent examples can be found in letters sent to those 'feedback' programmes so popular on the radio today. Most of the writers are firm for one ideological position or another (like that stock-figure 'Disgusted of Tunbridge Wells'); they have honed a style for their indignation almost entirely made up of phrases so worn with use that they have become deplorable cliches. They could very easily be put on a computer's floppy or hard disk for regular use. They are predictable, portentous and do not advance their arguments; they are packeted slogans, like insults hurled in a school playground or at Hyde Park Corner. It might be interesting to hear the broadcasters explain what principles of selection they use, and define what purpose they think they serve. We may be sure that some such phrase as 'the voice of the people' would be invoked; that could be in one sense true, or it might be yet another example of sub-democratic special pleading.

So we reach for tags out of that almost bottomless box which history, geography, age, and our social class have handed to us. We take refuge, without always realising that that is what we are doing, in adages, epigrams, maxims, apophthegms, proverbs, saws, sayings, truisms, commonplaces, mottoes, axioms, conventional locutions. There are differences between all these, but, for the purposes of this book, I will draw on all of them; they have much in common.

In *The Rotters' Club,* Jonathan Coe produces a painful parody of refuge-cliches from an abused husband: 'I said, "Barbara, we've reached a crossroads. This is the end of the road. It's him or me," I

said. "You have to choose between the devil and the deep blue sea."
I told her straight out. "You can't have your cake and eat it.'"

'And what did she say to that?'

'She told me to stop talking in cliches'.

Almost a quarter of a century ago, Eric Partridge was already list-
ing among newcomers several which remain in full rampant bloom
today, such as: 'In this day and age'. That must, he says, at first have
sounded sonorous and dignified, but by now 'implies mental de-
crepitude and marks a man for the rest of his life'. 'Its mentally
retarded offspring', he adds, is 'At this point in time'.

Sources

A very large number of adages in general use today have come,
often not much modified, from many centuries ago, especially from
Greek and Latin authors. Many also come from a long-gone rural
life, and draw on what was and sometimes still is regarded as undeniable folk wisdom—English, Scotch, Welsh and Irish wisdom, of
course—though many can be found across Europe and others even
much more widely. Folk wisdom can be more parochial in its thinking than in many of its origins.

No one in a packed working-class district of an English city in the
Thirties seemed to find anything archaic or out of place in the repeated invocations of horses (being led to water, etc.), cows (coming home), swallows (one not making a summer); or in the thought
of searching for a child 'up hill and down dale' or in declaring that
some belief or assumption is 'as old as the hills'. One need not assume that those who regularly asserted that something was 'as plain
as a pike-staff' had ever seen a pedlar with his pikestaff over his
shoulder; that image is at least five hundred years old. But perhaps
my grandmother had, as a girl in her then remote village, seen such
an itinerant.

Rural sayings are partnered by those from the Bible, by injunctions more often ethical than spiritual. This being Britain, some also
recall our imperial past, the wars and the soldiers and sailors who
fought them. One might call the Boer War the last pre-modern event
for the adding of many such images to the national pool, though
there are a few from the two world wars. When a fierce quarrel developed or 'blew up' in our house, we usually said as it intensified:
'the balloon's gone up'. Later, one might have assumed that the image was inspired by the barrage balloons over urban and industrial

areas in the Second World War. Obviously it was not, since we used it in the thirties. Its origins were in the battlefield observation balloons of the First World War.

Today's ubiquitous, unending, and overlapping forms of mass communication have produced their own kinds of pre-fabricated speech, especially in the form of 'sound-bites', which are meant to be briefly remembered, to stick in the mind awhile, but each of which, as is the nature of endlessly successive electronic communications in the service of persuasion, cannot last, must be if at all possible superseded. Are they, like some greedy growths that destroy all before them, going to succeed, take over from the slower but, so far, longer-lasting and hence more memorable accretions of the pre-modern period—until they are themselves pushed into oblivion?

Few of the more traditional phrases have come from books, but that is not surprising; most were born of oral not written use, passed from mouth to mouth. Interesting exceptions include 'itchy palm', which occurs in Shakespeare's *Julius Caesar* (but did he coin it?); 'Improve the shining hour' is in Isaac Watts's poem, 'How doth the little busy bee improve each shining hour', and it, too, may be older. The first is at least four centuries, the second at least two and a half centuries, old.

How were they transmitted to early 20th-century Hunslet? Isaac Watts's line sounds exactly like a Methodist precept of the sort we heard every week at Sunday School; it seems likely that Watts was our direct source. How did 'itchy palm' move up and along after Shakespeare?

Of the many epigrams from abroad, the largest group seem to be French and most of them apparently date from the Norman Conquest and after. The bad workman blaming his tools is found in late 13th-century French before appearing in English (*'mauves ovriers ne trovera ja bon hostill'*).

Given the difficulty of communications in the early days, there are more epigrams from the USA., some going back two centuries or more, than might have been expected. Since copyright was then weak or nonexistent there was from the early 19th century a brisk trade in both directions. The children of educated English families knew and loved some of the best novels, from New England and the Mid-West in particular. The soldiers of two world wars, films and television, greatly accelerated the process. Bill Bryson lists many unexpectedly North American imports, such as: 'having an axe to grind', 'having a chip on the shoulder', 'keeping a stiff upper lip' (even more surprising), 'pulling the wool over someone's eyes', and 'to whitewash' some act. That those and many another were adopted is not surprising; they are so often lively. Two we first met, when settling in there for a year in the mid-fifties, were: 'You're looking bright-eyed and bushy-tailed today' and 'You hit the land like a cat out of a sack'. Splendid. I have subsequently heard them both here, but each only two or three times so far.

There are also some from China and India; both have a special intriguing niche and the suggestion of very ancient wisdom. That there should be many from India is easily explained. But the Chinese? Probably some filtered through from the Opium trade. One wonders whether the Chinese have some illicitly fathered on them, especially if they suggest oriental wisdom, felt to be very different from and deeper than English. Variants of 'If I have two pennies I would spend one on bread and one on a rose', usually described as an old Chinese aphorism, pop up wherever someone is arguing for the public spending of more money on the arts in Britain. More cautious writers amend that to 'three pennies, two for bread, one for the arts', which might be thought to appeal more to British philistinism.

From wherever they come, most epigrams are used throughout society though not evenly distributed. Still, we may be said to have here something of a common culture: as English and British, to some extent also as Europeans, or simply as human beings. These are linguistic tap-roots for us all; but, importantly, each will have its different flavour.

Characteristics

Adages and their near-relatives run in all directions. They often contradict each other and leave us free to pick which suit us, according to taste or mood. We may solemnly warn a relative who is proposing to take a job far away that: 'A rolling stone gathers no moss', that 'East West. Home's best', that 'There's no place like home', and 'absence make the heart grow fonder'. Or, quite willing to see him or her go, we may cheerfully tell him that he does well not 'to let the grass grow/the dust gather/under his feet', that 'He who hesitates is lost'—but perhaps add the sombre 'out of sight is out of mind'.

That little group illustrates, incidentally, an earlier point about the wide historical spread of current commonplaces. In dates of origin they alone reach from the Greeks and Romans, the mid-13th and early 16ᵗʰ centuries; from Propertius and Hesiod to Erasmus and Addison. 'East West, Home's best' started in Germany. In these things we are all unconscious internationalists.

Many such sayings can be used on different occasions and in different contexts, and be true there, but, it follows, not be universally true or applicable. We tend to choose a relevant one and stick it on as a validation of how we feel at that moment, in that time and place. There are sayings for all seasons. They are not usually in themselves multipurpose; each normally has only one purpose at one time: reinforcement. Taken as a group, they are multiapplicable, because they can apply to quite different experiences. Many are likely to be repeated in different settings in the following chapters and should not be redundant in any of those places. The same ones will no doubt appear in discussions of work, neighbourliness, morals, poverty, and elsewhere; and sometimes contradict each other.

Their most common single characteristic is sententiousness; they sound like hall-marked truths, totally true currency, sage and safe finger-wagging; or self-satisfied and smug; sometimes would-be-wise saws with applicable modern instances. They seem as if drawn from a cistern of unassailable wisdom, and the more unassailable if they are or sound ancient. 'It never rains but it pours' sounds hardly worth saying and not true anyway; then one remembers Claudius speaking to Gertrude in *Hamlet*: 'When sorrows come, they come not single spies / But in battalions', which captures the memorable weight of sad experience.

They have withstood one test of time and so, often, have their like in single words. 'I can't abide (so-and-so or such-and-such...)' sounds truer than 'I can't stand [or 'put up with' or 'support']...'. In Yorkshire, 'thoil' ('thole' even further North—and, further back, of Indian origin) sounds firmer than 'bear' or 'tolerate'). Words like those may maintain their hold because they represent old-style stability, chiefly of conduct, before experience, which would otherwise always be in unhappy or unsettling flux.

Some sound banal, inexcusably incontrovertible, so that you feel like responding: 'So what?' But there is occasionally a semantic trick there; they may mean more than they seem to say. Someone may aver (that seems the right word here, or 'asseverate' might be pulled from hiding as even more suitable) that 'Blood is thicker than water.' Yes, it is; how unnecessarily obvious. Then listen more closely to instances of it being applied and it can take on a much more clouded tone; it can become a euphemism for any number of nasty attitudes and acts, used to protect a relative. It can be brought in to excuse lying to save your 'own flesh and blood' from jail, or to defend and promote another relative's shifty practices. In short, it can illustrate a bad side of family loyalty. Those are the sorts of context in which they were most often used in our area. Odd that the earliest recorded use in this form is early 19th century; it sounds very much older.

Epigrams can be brief, taut, witty: 'Easy come, easy go', (16th-century English, following mediaeval French), 'One law for the rich, another for the poor', 'Fine words butter no parsnips'. At moments adages such as those, and there are dozens, can seem for many of us suitably basic images which perfectly fit basic elements in living; they then deserve to be called 'memorable speech'. That may help to explain why, like hymns, they remain in our memories from when we first heard them in childhood to the end-part of our lives, even if that by now covers a very long time; they constantly surface or half-surface. But, being now educated and articulate, we no longer use many of them ourselves except in self-conscious inverted commas, and rarely hear them among the people with whom we now mix. Sometimes, yes. That last is a small particular habit of academics and other professionals who have emerged from the working class—when they are gathered together. It is like a totemic or Masonic signal, though used with a kind of amused recognition over all the years. A peer of the realm, born behind a corner-shop in a poor Sheffield area, and I used to drop into the ritual for a few minutes each time we met.

Very few of such epigrams are sophisticated; that is not the world they mainly belong to. Some, though, let people down lightly. This occurs particularly when they deal with death, health, sex and—intriguingly—any aspect of the intellectual life. Some, as we have seen, are witty, though that is not their predominant tone. Some sexual ones—for example, the one about 'not looking at the mantelpiece when you poke the fire', or 'A dirty mind is a perpetual feast'—sayings of that kind are as often witty as merely sniggering and coarse. Who would invent them? A witty person from the working class, and there are those in all classes, might have produced the mantelpiece motto. The 'perpetual feast' one is unusually polysyllabic; it sounds as if from a more than usually literate member of the working class though it may have been passed along or down from elsewhere. It was popular in Cockburn High School, introduced by a compulsive picker-up of smutty but funny sayings; perhaps he had invented it.

By now some coherences in speech of the Northern England working class of the twenties and thirties will be plain. But to conclude no more than that would be like plonking obliterating paint over a multicoloured if faded fresco. By the age of eight, in a curiously washed-up, almost classless part of north Leeds (most people there, young or old, were not well-off), and just off the wrong side of a main road out of town to the 'better' districts, I had certainly acquired an accent and type of speech more gentle than those of Hunslet; yet I cannot now identify any locution which came from there rather than from the migration at that age. Probably some did, but then merged with the Hunslet ones; protective colouring would have come into play so that I modified some, or at least the way they were said, and adopted others.

The new family included a grandmother who was in her early seventies, but still uttered adages more drawn from the Yorkshire rural peasantry than from the South Leeds working class. She must have left the village and her work in the Big Hall about 1880. Some of her turns of phrase would have long been in circulation in South Leeds, from the time when the first 'hands' of industry arrived there; at those workers' barracks created to house great numbers of immigrants from the country to the factories; row upon row going up cheaply and quickly, as if overnight, like mushrooms.

The elder aunt in the household, Clara, had worked for years at a 'good' women's outfitters in Huddersfield, and picked up there some sayings of the urban Yorkshire lower middle class or even middle class, especially those which might nourish her aspirations towards the genteel. To an outsider, though, she would in her accents have sounded overwhelmingly working class; what she thought of as a firm transition to something 'better' was to outsiders, especially Southerners, a mere patina.

Which recalls—this is a slight diversion—two wives of grammar-school teachers who attended an evening class in Goole, in the early fifties. They had pronunciations, intonations, even phrasings which seemed to them and others in the class clearly to distinguish them as being a slight step-up (as primarily their husband's jobs would also indicate, in that place at that time).

A process of unconscious filtration was going on there, in their hearing of themselves; and, they assumed, in that of others. One day

I brought into the class one of those new machines, a tape recorder. and recorded a few minutes of the class discussion, chiefly to indicate the ways in which a free discussion moved forward and back, and could develop, or not. The two ladies heard themselves for the first time and discovered that their voices sounded not at all 'cultivated' but, to their shocked ears, almost overwhelmingly 'Goole'; or at least as 'plain Northern'. They were greatly set back and left the class. This was, of course, before the BBC had begun to celebrate the variety and interest of regional speech. It would not likely have mollified them to be included in any such category. They wanted to speak 'properly' and thought they did; they did not want to be categorised as among local exhibits.

That bypass beckoned when Aunt Clara's modes of speech were being looked at. She used what she liked to think of as some forms of speech better, more polite, than those of Hunslet—to which she had finally returned—and with newer pronunciations to match. As to what mainly concerns us here, the sayings rather than the pronunciations, she had taken over a few which we otherwise would not have heard. She would say, if she became impatient, that something was 'much ado about nothing'. We did not use that, and neither Clara nor the rest of us (at least not till I went to grammar school) were likely to know that it was from Shakespeare, or before. She would have heard it in the shop, from her seniors or from customers. She did not say: 'There's method in his madness', or use any other lines from Shakespeare which are commonly used 'higher up'.

Her younger sister, Lil, had a naturally developed ear for language, especially for striking images. That resurfaced in our sister Molly. Both of them could pass a group of women 'calling' (the flat 'calling' = gossiping, and is not pronounced 'corling') in the street and pick up, like sparrow hawks on the wing, juicy phrasings. 'Eh, do you know what she said then...?' was the preamble as the morsel was dropped into our laps. No others in the house, except perhaps her brother Herbert, recognised Aunt Lil's gift for speech—not 'the gift of the gab' but a natural response to metaphor (usually overheard), the entrance-gate to creativity in language.

Uncle Herbert's working-life revolved round the cheapish furniture store in which he was a salesman and the city centre bars he frequented most evenings before heading for home. His livelier phrasings were those of raffish-talkative-joke-cracking-lower-middle-class-shop-assistants rather than of the working class, and didn't on the whole go down well in the house. That is another intriguing side-alley, but not one about which I can recall much.

Last in the Newport Street family was Ivy, the refugee from the Sheffield Means Test Man. She had some Sheffield pronunciations; for one, the glottal stop seemed less evident there than in Leeds, but she spoke little. How acute one's ear was at the time to slight local differences in speech. To us, Ivy unmistakably 'spoke Sheffield' but, apart from the glottal stops, those different nuances are now forgotten.

Ivy was not surly or withdrawn; phlegmatic, rather, and so apart emotionally from the fights which regularly went on in that house; her heart was back in her crowded Sheffield home—Mum, Dad and still six or seven unmarried others—and then, after she met her Alf, with him. From then, her aim was simply to get back to Sheffield and to take Alf with her. She managed that. Her general air—her almost silent aura—was of a firm, unaggressive and not unpleasant separateness, with no striking manner or idioms. I do not recall one memorable phrase from her.

Outside were the streets and the boys who, especially, roamed them; they had an argot of their own, usually more vulgar than we heard at home and much preoccupied with bodily functions and sex. In any sizeable group of boys there was likely always to be one with an ear for felicities in speech. He could both himself create, and be a 'gatekeeper' for, a carrier of, locutions from outside; he let in the more attractive—in the group's terms. There were also, in this, fine distinctions. After I had been at grammar school for a year or two, the other boys in the street recognised that I 'spoke better' and had a larger vocabulary; they did not assume without other evidence that I was one of the wittily gifted ones. That competition was different and not easily entered.

Leeds University produced its own adages, not intentionally but by its mixture of students. Those with scholarships were predominantly working or lower middle class, as distinct from medics, engineers and students of textiles in all their forms, who came from higher-up socially and usually had fathers successful in those professions round about the West Riding, or far afield, on other continents.

Most of us were linguistically quite lively, but deliberately did not much display our backgrounds through our speech; we were busy discovering new linguistic habits, particularly if they had a snook-cocking element. All that went into the mix. We might by that time have learned to say, jocularly, that one's 'withers were unrung' by some set-back. That phrase certainly did not come from Hunslet and may not have been picked up from reading *Hamlet*. It was only one example of new phrases acquired on the way out and up.

After I met Mary, who became my wife, there was added from 1937 a number of Stalybridge working-class idioms; those were close to Hunslet's, but had some different seasonings. All in all, many of my kind became polyglot-shuttlers, up and down and sideways, linguistically.

All that helped to give to each part of our own thesauruses of epigrams and the like its peculiar character, in the early years chiefly according to the differences between individual families within our rather closed group. The group within a group. The Hoggarts were above all 'respectable', protestant and puritanical, firmly anti-vulgarity, non-political except for many conservative—rather than Conservative—instincts; we did not vote, not really expecting to 'get on' but very anxious not to sink.... One could go on and on here.

Preeminently, those qualities inclined us, both those who stayed within the group and those who were on the way out, towards which of the huge vocabulary of working-class maxims we would use most and with what force. The differences between families throughout the one street were slight. In some other streets, perhaps occupied mainly by people who had 'gone downhill', or by families who had long been 'no better than they should be', the differences could be much greater.

Almost six years with a cockney regiment during the war revealed that the bulk of working-class idioms were common to Northerners and Southerners. The cockneys had some of their own, drawn mainly from a vigorously combative and resilient attitude to life, especially towards work and women and class differences, an attitude stronger and more readily and radically expressed than anything similar in Hunslet. They had more recognised 'jokers', 'wits', in any group than we could take for granted. They were verbally inventive 'on the hoof', as a matter of tradition, especially if sex had 'reared its ugly head ' and given irresistible grounds for a joke. Getting ready to enter Tunis after months in the desert we held a parade to hand out precautionary 'French letters'. One gunner affected to be bewildered and pretended to be trying to inflate his: 'What are these for, then, Sarge?' Before the sergeant could speak another voice gave the answer: 'For tossing yerself off on Sundays'. Brilliant, dry, mockingly-unexpectant.

'That's all water under the bridge', slightly shimmering with the suggestion that we should leave the past alone and also that succeeding things now face us, is one of those epigrams common to all classes; and by now over-tired. Its rural nature, together with that of many others such as 'Time and Tide wait for no man' and 'Rain before seven, fine before eleven', recalls a period when master and man communed on the weather and work, or mistress and maid on the business of housekeeping. They spoke mutually.

It is harder to identify with certainty sayings that have filtered down socially, though that must have happened; we will no doubt meet some on the way. Others are almost peculiar to a class, since they speak directly to that class's particular experiences and may be expressed in class language. There may be barriers of education and sophistication, of occupation and of leisure against further floating off and down. Or even up? Obviously, working-class people will have few aphorisms about commerce, the market, bargaining, lawyers, estate agents; they will have many about wages, bosses, football and Football Pools (and, now, the National Lottery), rent, the dole, the debt-collector and workmates. A working-class man is unlikely to announce that he is 'bust', 'bankrupt' or, even less likely, has been 'hammered' on the Stock Exchange. He may say that, as a result of taking out too many Hire Purchase agreements, he is 'skint', hasn't 'a penny to his name' (and may have fallen into the hands of loan-sharks). Drinking language is notably class-divided.

Some time ago, BBC Radio 4 broadcast a programme that reported favourite unusual remarks for recurrent situations, in different families. One was from a household in which, when they were behind-hand with the morning's chores, the mother would exclaim: 'Heavens! Eleven o'clock. And not a whore stirring!' Funny very *Guardian*-readerish; too vulgar for our sort of people. The response to the programme revealed that that saying was used in many non-working-class families, in interestingly different forms (and with additions such as 'and the Spanish/Japanese Fleet just in port').

Naturally, working-class people had a wide range of sayings about being poor; that is the theme of chapter 2. They also had many sayings about 'neighbourliness'. Middle-class people have more about 'friendship', though neighbourliness ranks high with them also. Working-class people seemed and seem to have more about superstition, fate, luck. chance. This does not necessarily imply that, in general, they look at horoscopes or read about the predictions in the stars, or patronise the National Lottery, more than do middle-class people. In some respects, middle-class people are as much 'caught up with' superstitious attitudes as working-class. From the evidence of the maxims themselves and from experience as a listener on both sides, it seems that working-class people do *talk* about such things more; and the tabloid newspapers predictably illustrate those subjects more often and more garishly than the broadsheets.

The great interest among working-class people in the workings of chance probably has much to do with the lack of perspective in their lives, with the restraining fact that life does not usually provide a ladder of possibilities, of promptings to ambition, for themselves or their children; that it is, rather, a flat movement along the years, not in any way to be called a 'progression'.

Some working-class people have more vulgar expressions than, in general, do middle-class people. Certain readers may almost instinctively take exception to this statement. That would be a pity. A little time hanging around building sites, bars in relevant areas, factories and football grounds will illustrate the truth of the statement. Even today many working-class people (between 15 and 20 percent are the latest figures) are not educated to a level of adequate literacy; many have hard and repetitive jobs. What do we expect? The 're-spectable' working class and the lower-middle class make a special point of avoiding vulgarity; that is one of their boundary-markers.

We have to jump to the upper-classes to find a different kind of vulgarity in speech, one that rejects gentility and asserts its ties with the land. The phrase 'in pig' for 'being pregnant' is typical. I heard it first, spoken quite unabashedly by a Cabinet Minister's aristocratic wife about her daughter, in the early seventies. Green's *Dictionary of Slang* dates it from 1940, and that may be the first recorded instance in print. Neither the early *Brewer* nor *Farmer and Henley* list it, though that may be due to the prudishness of the time. It is hard to believe that it was coined only half-way through the 20th century.

All in all, the old assumption is true: that the middle classes (with the lower-middle classes in support) provide a verbal chastity belt between the lower-lowers and the upper-uppers.

Manifestly, middle-class sayings will tend to be more polysyllabic, more referential, more aware of being 'well-educated', than could be expected from those who have not had such advantages. Working-class people would not say that they were 'on the horns of a dilemma' (nor, for that matter, would most of the middle-class people who might just possibly use it be likely to know that it came from Greek Rhetoric). Only a pompous and showing-off middle-class person would say, except ironically, that something 'Out Heroded Herod'. 'Holier than thou' might be shared by most classes, since it comes from both the Old and the New Testaments; but it was hardly heard in our part of Leeds. 'The iron has entered my soul' is also biblical, but who in any social group would seriously use it today? There is more than one process of filtration; this one is at least partly fed by the modern dislike of 'big bow-wow' speech and the decline of belief. More useable, probably starting in the middle class and also moving down, to some slight extent, are the early 17th-century: 'Don't let's split hairs', and the mid-19th-century: 'A safe pair of hands'. But both were rarely heard in Hunslet, and the second even less often than the first.

Perhaps it will be possible to produce by the end of this book a pictorial sketch of the phrases used by working-class people, according to frequency and emphasis. Perhaps one of those sketches which look on the page like a sliced orange? Or perhaps not. At one point I had thought also of putting a 'c' after phrasings common to all classes and a 'w' for those used particularly by working-class people. But that would disrupt the flow, and be textbookish. Most readers, from whatever class, will recognise those they use or have heard among their own kind, and will note the unusual.

Bundles and Clusters

We looked in the first pages here at the ground-base of all this; at pre-fabricated, hopscotch speech. That kind of speech is further held together by the clustering of phrases that share the same metaphorical objects. It is as though a painter had recurrent favoured images and colourings, which he incorporated in most of his pictures.

It should cause no surprise that 'water' forms the basis of many of these images; bread and water are as universal as it is possible for *things* to be. Water just wins over bread, as may be seen from a glance at the great number of water images recorded in any big dictionary.

Yet 'bread', even more homely, is a good second and its images march along, picking up numbers from the Greek, Latin, the Bible, and mediaeval literature, through to the USA. 'Earning your bread and butter', 'Knowing which side your bread is buttered' (a dour expression and common in our area), 'Casting your bread upon the

waters' and its biblical brother 'Man cannot live by bread alone'—
with us the first two appeared often, the third rarely, and the fourth
on Sundays, sometimes. 'He is taking the bread from my mouth'
was also and obviously frequent; but one did not hear about 'bread
and circuses'. 'A bread and butter' letter began in the lower-middle
class and has come from America.

'Salt', again homely and obvious, appeared often, though not 'below the salt'. We greatly liked to speak of 'the salt of the earth', to
say 'I took that with a pinch of salt', and fairly often talked of someone 'rubbing salt into the wound', or as not 'being worth his salt'.
Salt was also, as it has long been, associated with superstition. If we
spilt salt, we always and immediately threw more salt over our left
shoulder—with our right hand. Classical or biblical, all. In some
areas that throw to the left is thought to be aimed directly at the
Devil.

A mild surprise among sayings adopted from cottage'y use is the
recurrence of deeply rural 'ducks'. If you expected duck-aphorisms
to be more common in the country than the town you would probably be mistaken. They form another group which has survived te-
naciously, almost unchanged, throughout country-to-town movements. They survive in the urban metaphor-using consciousness,
even more than horses or dogs.

We have 'dying ducks', 'lame ducks', 'playing ducks and drakes';
we speak of picking up, taking to, some skill 'like a duck to water',
about rebukes having as much effect as 'water off a duck's back',
and of escape—from a personal challenge, it may be—by 'ducking
and diving' (which could take its name from the constant up-and-
down movement of a duck's head).

It seemed surprisingly archaic to hear a senior civil servant from a
major Ministry, in the late-seventies, negotiating closely with one he
took to becoming at least slightly over-insistent: 'Now, that cock
won't fight, Hodgkin'! By what routes did that come down over the
years? And how, by 2002, did a senior civil servant feel able to say
'fuck' and the Chaplain of an Oxford college to say 'shit' ? There's
a leap.

Taken together, as a mixed group, images of the body probably
outnumber even 'water' images. 'Bone' images are often slightly
sinister or gloomy, as in 'working my fingers to the bone', being
'chilled to the bone' or 'pared to the bone', 'making no bones about
it' (straight talking, or accepting without opposition), 'too near the

bone/knuckle' (usually something verging on the obscene), 'a bone of contention' and 'I have a bone to pick with you' (inspired by the sight of quarrelling dogs?). 'Bred in the bone' can point in two opposing directions, as to good or ill genetic influences on character.

Blood and bones. Blood joins bones in frequency. 'Blood is thicker than water' we have looked at already; it partners 'My own flesh and blood'. 'You can't get blood out of a stone' is one of poverty's mottoes. 'That sort of thing makes my blood boil' and 'My blood is up again' (both common in our household, but so was the reverse 'my blood ran cold'). 'There's bad blood between them' was a neighbourhood saying, alluding, of course, to a lack of 'neighbourliness'.

Then the appendages or constituent parts. The eyes, as in: 'Keeping your eye on' someone, especially if they show signs of 'having an eye on the main chance', a characteristic you claim to be able to recognise 'with half an eye', being good at detecting 'eye-wash'. Courtship involves 'Giving the glad eye' or 'Making eyes at'; 'Clapping eyes on someone' may suggest an accidental but usually not altogether happy occurrence. You may 'Shut your eyes to' a demeanour or action you don't want to make a fuss about, even though you can see that they are undesirable. The line goes on and on; especially on the need to make full use of your eyes, as in 'He's all eyes', 'He has eyes in the back of his head' (or 'needs eyes in the back of his head'). You may be 'Up to your eyes in work' but still have to 'Keep your eyes well open'. 'All my eye and Betty Martin' is comical and intriguing, but even the biggest Oxford English Dictionary fails to identify her. It does name an admiral who was given to the phrase. Perhaps he indicated by it something quite useless, as it might be a preposterous opinion or excuse from a subordinate.

Ears appear roughly as often as eyes. We may be habitually inattentive, so that things 'Go in at one ear, out at the other', or be 'Cloth-eared' or 'Thick-eared' or listen with only 'Half an ear'. For that, we may even be given 'A flea in our ear' or even 'Thrown out on our ear'. Alternatively, we may 'Have an ear to the ground', or be 'All ears'. Our hopeful plan may be 'Brought down about our ears' so that we become 'Up to our ears' in debt. The impossibility of 'making a silk purse out of a sow's ear' has come down from at least the early 16th-century, and 'Your ears must be burning' is very much older; most here are some centuries old.

The mouth figures much less often. Many of those sayings are unhappy, are 'Down in the mouth', such as 'Don't put words into my mouth' and 'I gave them a mouthful'. On the other hand, some things can be 'mouth-watering' and a gift horse should not be 'Looked in the mouth'. Out in the streets but not in our house it might be said that someone, a thoroughly unpleasant gossip for instance, was 'all mouth and no knickers'.

Out of the body, the Devil has a clear lead. Especially in nastiness, as in 'There'll be the Devil to pay', 'Between the Devil and the deep blue sea', 'That's the Devil's own job', and 'Needs must when the Devil drives', 'The Devil looks after his own', 'Sup with the Devil, but use a long spoon'. On the other hand, 'Better the Devil you know' and 'Give the Devil his due'. The old Devil still holds much of his force. Today's M. P.'s are fond of : 'The Devil is in the detail'; and one wonders why. Habit, or a faint but persistent echo? Or simply alliteration?

Then, one adjective and one element. 'Thick' is popular: we can offer a 'thick ear' to a rude child, after his behaviour has been 'A bit thick'. Problems can come 'Thick and fast' when we are in 'The thick of things'. We can be 'As thick as thieves' with someone, but friends such as that will never be 'Thick on the ground'. 'As thick as two short planks' is several centuries old; two decades ago Princess Diana described herself to a passing acquaintance in that way. 'Through thick and thin' is one of the few which straddles both conditions. 'Thin' as in 'Thin-skinned', 'Thin air', 'Thin on the ground', 'Thin ice', 'The thin end of the wedge', and 'Having a thin time of it' are a few from a not very large number.

'Time', mentioned above, brings us to the element which most figures in these clusters. Not surprisingly, it comes up everywhere. 'Time and tide wait for no man', 'Time out of mind', 'In the nick of time', 'Taking time by the forelock', 'From time immemorial', 'Time will tell', 'Time is a great healer', 'There's a time and a place for everything' (much used by Protestants), 'Third time pays for all'.

'Time' lives in that part of our collective memories that pays homage to Superstition, Luck, the Stars, Fate and Chance, as something to which we like to give primordial powers. Respect for it, fear of it, hope from it, endures and will endure.

*   *   *

This whole enterprise begins to seem like a sort of verbal weaving, of textures, colours, shades, backwards, in several directions of time and space. It is inevitable, and already worth repeating, that some idioms will recur in more than one context, and so will the elements that inspired each appearance. Thus, to take only one such particular element, that lack of an upward perspective in working-class life is relevant not only to poverty but also to neighbourliness, class, tolerance and belief in the workings of Fate.

2

Poverty and Its Languages

One's only got to look at the hopeless dreary expression on the faces of poor people to realise what it [poverty] must be.
                                   —Nancy Mitford, The Road to Wigan Pier

We are mistaken when we say that "It isn't the same for them as it would be for us," and that people bred in the slums can imagine nothing but the slums. For what I saw in her face was not the ignorant suffering of an animal. She knew well enough what was happening to her...
                                   —George Orwell, The Road to Wigan Pier

The Nature of Poverty

Nancy Mitford's novel was published in 1949, but treats of earlier English life, seen here by one of her characters. It is true to one way of viewing working-class people in the thirties: from the perspective of an aristocratic woman who is for most of the time horribly snobbish, but here shows some sympathetic understanding. Curiously, because from an opposite viewpoint, it reminds us of George Orwell's *The Road to Wigan Pier*. Both home in on *expressions* of hopelessness. Orwell's eye is more pictorial, less distanced and generalised; he focuses on a poor housewife trying to unblock a drain on the outside of her miserable house.

Since we express our worlds—our needs and desires, our senses of loss or success, and our reactions to all such feelings—through our mouths, through our languages, that process is part personal, part collective, and not entirely conscious. So, to recall what is described in the preceding chapter as the main theme of this book, it is right to assume that our favoured idioms will reflect the key elements, the compelling conditions of life, for all of us whatever our time and place. For the British working class before the last war that over-arching element was poverty, poverty with varying degrees of severity.

Today, when we do not like any longer to speak of 'the working class' and sometimes deny that it still exists, we are uneasy about giving a name to its smaller, but evidently worse-off successor. The word 'underclass', the most honest description we have so far been offered, is generally rejected as patronising, belittling. That refusal is regrettable; the word accurately pinpoints the position of those who have replaced the pre-war working class, who are indeed and in fact belittled; it recognises a truth many of us do not wish fully to acknowledge. We try to escape from what it is telling us. Few who are living there find escape, getting out from under, easy.

To what extent does that 'underclass', today's really poor, still use its condition phrasings employed by or similar to those of its predecessor? The differences between the two ways of life are enormous. Those in the pre-war working class were largely born into that state and most did not leave it. They were a much larger and more varied group than today's underclass. They covered a wide range of types of poverty and of capacities for coping. Not all were 'poverty-stricken', 'ground down', but many were; and many, at times most, were influenced by the thought of the extreme threat of deprivation through being sacked. Most even among those lucky enough to be in work knew on which side 'their bread was buttered' and knew that that well-worn phrase threatened a dire possibility and glossed the reality; their bread was as like as not thinly spread with margarine; and unemployment often loomed.

Those in today's 'underclass', though they may be offered money from Social Security to an extent that could have seemed generous to their predecessors, even after allowing for differences in the value of money and the cost of living, have been markedly 'separated out', winnowed like chaff from a mindless machine, are to some extent uniform in their severe wants, have been born outside or fallen out of a society in which most others of the earlier working class have become increasingly prosperous. For them, the newer nets have not held; they have become progressively worse-off by comparison with society as a whole. They may be a smaller percentage of that whole or than the older working class were. They are even more enclosed and at the same time less sustained by a surrounding group in the same condition, or by opportunities of rewarding work.

The one-parent family, that parent usually a woman, living on a run-down council housing estate, may be taken as the prototype of that group. Insofar as they do use well-worn phrases about their condition, and that is inevitable, many of those phrases seem likely to have some different characteristics—force, underlying emotion— from the uses of their forerunners. It is easy to guess that among them many of the old sayings remain, used much as they always were. Nevertheless, the two situations are hardly comparable; today's poverty-stricken live on the often fragmented and submarine margins, in a very different world from that of their parents and grandparents. Above all it is, to underline again, a world that can offer much less of a sense of community, of neighbourliness.

*   *   *

It should not be surprising that very quickly from the depths of memory someone from a working class background can retrieve well over a hundred common idioms about the ever-present reality of being poor in the thirties, about the many kinds of straitened circumstances, the struggle for survival, the effort to 'make ends meet'. How vivid that becomes when you look closely at it—as does the need to 'keep your head above water', to avoid drowning. Many lived 'from hand to mouth' (that almost five- century-old epigram is arrestingly economical—if meagre food came in for the poorest, it was, it had to be, eaten at once. No refrigerators. It might soon 'go off', and who knew 'where the next meal was coming from'?). Many deployed such counters, like worn chips in a game they were committed, condemned to playing day after day. They were a major part of their regular and repetitive living—and linguistic—experiences.

Today few remember or ever knew that the Old Age Pension only came in with the Liberal Government of 1906, not really very long ago, or that most of the greatly feared 'Workhouses' for penniless old people lingered until 1939, and that a few lasted until just after the Second World War. That threat had hung like a spectre over the really poor and old for many decades. 'Whatever happens, don't let Them put us in the Workhouse', was a regular plea from old grandparents. Only the self-regarding or those who really had no spare space allowed that to happen to their parents. Today there are many Old People's Homes, some privately owned, some owned by local authorities. Some are good, some not; there is still often guilt when an elderly relative is consigned to even a good home. Those feelings can be slightly assuaged by visits on Sunday, unless other interests get in the way—such as children's demands to go somewhere more interesting.

Before the war, all such experiences of the intricacies of poverty were repeatedly, endlessly, routinely put in play as group-locutions; often in very old forms; sometimes used only for phatic communion, and sometimes as if new-minted, when a particular experience hit home with exceptional force. One of the mildest, 'hard up', is at least two centuries old; 'poor as church mice' announces its own long derivation; as do 'scraping the barrel' and 'at the end of my tether'. That last word is one whose origins—from an animal, probably a goat, reaching the end of the rope by which it is tethered to a post—few employing it nowadays could be expected to know.

Inevitably, the image of a prolonged and draining fight came up again and again. It was a fight to 'keep body and soul together', even to 'keep the wolf from the door'. If you were successful in that, after long deprivation, you were no doubt tempted to 'wolf' your food. Generally, you were, to move to an adopted nautical expression, 'on your beam-ends' and knew what that meant but, again, probably not where it came from. Much more accessible were direct phrases of the day-by-day: 'not a penny to my name', 'not two ha'pence to rub together', 'not a penny to bless myself with'; 'in Queer Street', 'on my uppers'.

Your kids might be always 'out at elbow' and not see 'a square meal' from one weekend to another ('square' is odd, and rarely explained. Apparently it emerged from the USA in the early 19th century, and means "substantial"). Did it derive from the shape of some plates designed to hold a full dish, meat and vegetables and all? Were the children 'eating you out of house and home', so that you warned them to: 'take what you're given' if they proved 'picky' with their food. Against such a barrage the middle-class expression 'in reduced circumstances' sounds genteel, defensively purse-lipped.

That earlier 'making ends meet' is by comparison remarkably exact. If the ends didn't meet you couldn't manage. Put another way: you had no room for manoeuvre, no 'play' in your weekly money, no 'elbow room.' This recalls an obvious but little recognised truth: that for a wife (it being usually the wife who ran the household and its funds) in a poor household managing was, in the thirties, and is today or at any time, more difficult than for a wife with a little bit left over at the end of each week. The Micawber model: you had to have 'a tight hold on the purse-strings', or else.... A broken gas-mantle or light bulb could cause a perceptible wobble in the week's reckonings; the realisation that a child's shoes needed replacing could bring near shipwreck. Grandma was clearly worried about some unexpected expense if in a rather muted way she told me, setting out with a list to do the Friday evening shopping, to ask the grocer if we could have 'tick', carry at least part of our debt over for a week. He never demurred; he knew he could trust our household memory.

A housewife shocked by a light left on unnecessarily, and expostulating—'don't waste daylight'—need not have been mean but would, rather, always be worried about keeping that tight balance. No wonder the 'Clubs'—usually offering clothing and some household goods through payment by instalments, and run by local women on behalf of big mail-order firms—filled a threatening gap. Rates of interest on 'Club cheques' did not seem exorbitant. The loan sharks of today are a growing band, since we are all constantly urged to buy and told that borrowing is easy, but not told that the rates of interest are punitive. For many in the underclass this is the chief current threat. Today the Mercedes of the Boss-loan-shark, waiting just outside the area being milked for that week by his underlings, is a typical and telling sight.

The 'Clubs' have not disappeared; one at least operates today in the council housing-estate just over the road from us and caters not only to the hard-up but to working wives with some money to spare, widened tastes and not much time to 'shop around'. For them the goods on offer are colourful and modern, stylish; ours were more down to earth.

The Co-ops. come in here, and their brilliant invention, 'The Divvi' (Dividend). That rather resembled, say, Sainsbury's 'Rewards' scheme of today. You, as the equivalent of a shareholder, earned something for each pound spent. Every time you shopped you gave the assistant your Co-op. Number (known by heart, almost always) and were handed a very small, thin, perforated slip which you stuck to a gummed sheet. When 'Divvi time' came round each half-year you cashed all those. For most families this was the only windfall, unless they won something on the Pools (those had been launched in the early twenties). It often came as 'a godsend', long waited for when debts were growing; or children needed new clothes, especially at Whitsuntide.

We were not 'in the Co-op'. We were so respectable that we sort-of-assumed membership of the Co-op. was slightly beneath us, perhaps even a bit socialistic; we weren't 'Co-op. people'. That feeling certainly existed, but probably was not widely held. Had we also discovered that the Sunshine Grocers, which we did patronise, were a few pence cheaper than the Co-op. for most staples? That could well have been so and could have decided the question.

For many of us brought up in such circumstances, and who nowadays have 'a bit left over' each week or month, to spend some money almost casually can still seem more than casual—nearly wanton. To bring some flowers or a bottle of wine home on a whim, to suggest going out for a pub lunch, or making a trip to the Sales simply to see what might be picked up, all these can still give a sensuous pleasure, with a tinge of puritanical guilt: 'waste not, want not'; 'you'll pay for this'.

Putting up with Poverty

In those earlier days, reactions naturally differed. The most common, the core, attitude was to 'put up with it all', to 'go on going on'. That had three main ways of expressing itself, varying according to a person's health, the extent of the problem (that itself determined mainly by the size of the family and perhaps the husband's behaviour, whether he was a boozer, the support he gave about the house) and native resilience. Some, inevitably more wives than husbands since day-by-day working-things-out usually fell to them, became depressed and often sighed that 'it never rains but it pours', that 'misfortunes never come singly', that life is certainly not 'all beer and skittles'. They 'threw up their hands', talked of 'the cross we have to bear' in 'this vale of tears', exclaimed that 'you can't get blood out of a stone', or that some other people 'don't know they're born', being comfortably off in comparison with the speaker. 'There's one law for the rich and one for the poor'; and of course 'beggars can't be choosers'. 'It'll always be 'jam tomorrow, but never jam today'. They might become convinced that to seek to mend things or to hope for outside help towards a better life was 'like banging your head against a brick wall', and that they couldn't much longer 'put off the evil hour' when they might have to seek help from one of the Offices in town, or even go down to the pawnshop, or expect the rent man to become threatening, or the bailiffs to appear on the doorstep. Some but by no means all were practised exponents of the: 'They ought to do this ...' principle, 'They' being the 'powers-that-be'. Our widowed mother never dropped into that mode; she would have thought it 'beneath her'. Life at the bottom was hard enough, but you didn't automatically have to look for others entirely to blame.

Without lacking concern for people in such plights, one always felt sad when, in response to some call on even them for help no matter how small, a few were driven to reply that 'charity begins at home'; a denial of the nature of charity and of Good Samaritans' practice (which was likely, there, to be praised in other circumstances, and by some of the same people, when they were the recipients).

That kind of family, the habitually complaining group in a characteristically mixed working-class district—some in good work, some in less well-paid work, some unemployed, some retired and just about coping—would usually be in a minority though its proportion of the whole in the streets round about would vary from time to time, altering as industry prospered or lacked orders. The very hard-up group included the out-of-work, many of the old, the disabled or sick, the deserted wives, and the 'feckless'. The more fortunate but still not really prosperous larger group would 'go-on-going-on', 'putting up with' circumstances, 'keeping their heads above water', full of wise or trite saws about their condition but not continually grumbling about it; or seeking someone to blame; or actually falling below the true poverty line.

Their central range of attitudes did not include much 'kicking against the pricks' but most of the time expressed the determination to 'soldier on'. It accepted that there was no use in 'crying over spilt milk", that 'we're all in the same boat' (which implicitly invokes the dues of neighbourliness), that it's 'Hobson's choice' for us. Hobson, a 17th-century innkeeper of Cambridge, gave no choice of horses when you hired from him. You had to take the next one in his line. It is odd that, from dozens, that particular old idiom should stick so firmly in the folk memory. Was Hobson proud of every horse in his rotating line, or merely stiff and stubborn?

Two contradictory saws were often used without hint of contradiction: 'All good things come to an end' and 'Everything comes to him who waits' (meant hopefully). We will meet such pairs again. Many live in separate compartments and rarely clash, to cause embarrassment.

You 'made do', 'put up with' the 'swings and roundabouts' of life. It would be too much to say that 'you pays your money and you takes your choice' since, not having much money, you have never had much of a choice; strange, then, that that expression was so frequently used. Perhaps it recognised that you did after all have *some* freedom, that there were still some choices to be made, and they might be good or bad; you *could* decide that. Against this background, there might then be invoked yet another biblical echo—'All such things are sent to try us'. So we should 'possess our souls in patience;' and 'get on with it'.

This range of more stoical choices is exceptionally long: 'What can't be cured must be endured', 'make the best of a bad job' (half-cousin to 'make do and mend' which more often has a very practical application, though it can be used metaphorically), 'It's no use crying over spilt milk/for the moon', 'you have to swallow a peck of dirt before you die' (also useable in other contexts); and, recalling two in the large Devil cluster, 'better the Devil you know' (to justify staying with a bad boss, for example) and 'needs must when the Devil drives'. So they run on: 'What's done can't be undone', 'nothing so bad but might have been worse', 'you can't get a quart from a pint pot' (in managing the family's money), 'what the eye doesn't see the heart doesn't grieve' (that has a huge range of self-vindicating applications, from those which excuse a tiny error to the most inexcusable—such as adultery); 'if you don't like it you'll have to lump it', 'it'll all be the same in a hundred years' time' and, slightly more encouraging, after a typically plain meal, 'Enough is as good as a feast'. Finally, for now: 'money isn't everything' (well, no. Yet one learned to say to oneself: 'All the same, it can go a long way; it helps'). As that undeniable-sounding tide rolled on, that insistence on a 'tough as old boots' stoicism, one began to weary and wish to shout: 'Bite the backsides of those above you. Don't just "put up" with it'.

On the other hand, steadily 'putting up' with the hand you have been dealt can be above all an expression of self-respect. We may be poor but...we try to live decent lives; and we are clean. For some, cleanliness can become an obsession, a puritanical fetish. 'Cleanliness is next to godliness'; what an enormous jump! And often unpleasant—as in the fanaticism of Nora Batty (in BBC television's Northern situation comedy, *The Last of the Summer Wine*), always 'yellowing' the steps or swilling down the flags, and daring/glaring her neighbours to do likewise, just as thoroughly. It is the world of scouring anything in sight which can be subjected to that process, of rough carbolic soap being used on a remarkably large range of objects, from dirty floor-boards to boys' dirty faces; of rug-bashing against walls; of the clamped hold on respectability, of having a constant ear to 'what the neighbours might think'. For such people the definition of the phrase 'house-proud' reaches a new depth; of forbiddingness. 'Clean' has its dire opposite in 'mucky'; like 'tasty', 'mucky ' is one of the most meaningful—multi-meaningful—words in the working-class vocabulary.

The reputed belief among some middle-class people, that if you put baths in council houses the tenants would keep coals in them, was ludicrously off the point (though an elderly French aristocratic lady in our apartment building in Paris offered something similar to that as the justification for not providing a bath on the top floor, for those in the *chambres de bonnes*. What those Portuguese servants would have put in the bath, since coal was not used in that building, was an intriguing question. Perhaps rough red plonk or live sardines. The only consideration that would have stopped some of our neighbours from having frequent baths—and it would, of course, have been a major factor—would have been the cost of heating the water. The more frugal Friday ritual, among many, of giving themselves a sort of bath, an 'all-over' wash, had a strong hold, both economical and affectionate.

Our house, being at a terrace-end and boasting an attic, had a free-standing, painted-iron bath up there, with a clothes-horse draped in wallpaper standing on duty to protect privacy. Daughters of neighbours used our bath on the eve of their weddings. Did we charge for heating the water? Probably not, though later some small gift might have been offered. Ourselves, we had a Friday night 'proper' bath; but in an economical depth of water. When council houses began to include a bathroom, sharing water between husband and wife was, when they were young, common; amiable and economical. For me later, one of the more striking introductions to middle-class habits was that of the daily bath; also sometimes shared by younger couples, though not out of parsimony.

For those who 'thought well of themselves', cleanliness was, had to be, a part of 'keeping your end up'; of the constant struggle. Most heavy labour was dirty labour; the atmosphere full of the detritus of factory chimneys, but the commercial cleaning of clothes cost too much for anything other than very occasional use. The social historian H. L. Beales remarked that a characteristic smell of working-class life in the twenties and thirties was that of wet clothes huddled in a tramcar on a rainy night. He could have added that, late in the evening, the smell of beer joined in; and, upstairs, of Woodbines.

In this light an adage which most of us normally assume applies to gossip and indiscreet confession—'Don't wash your dirty linen in public'—could acquire literal force. Hanging your washing out on the line across the street was a public exposure; had you 'bottomed it', got all the grime out? Revealing dirty linen would never do. A favourite comic injunction becomes emblematic. If you are going on a trip into town, say, 'make sure you've got clean knickers on'. If you are run over and taken to hospital no one there (curious locution) *'wants to see'* your dirty knickers. One wonders how many took that literally. Perhaps very few; but the image certainly touched a nerve in the collective local culture, and was used in the lower-middle and, to some extent, middle class.

Related to all said so far, about 'putting up with things', 'making the best of it', is the realisation that all such attitudes rest in the deep-rooted sense of unexpectancy. We noted in the first chapter that for working-class people life did not and for many still does not, offer a ladder; instead it offers a permanent seat on an old-fashioned roundabout or a carousel, though not a particularly cheerful ride on either. There were few opportunities or openings. When we were orphaned and spread around parts of our working class extended family, our brother Tom was sent to an aunt in Sheffield who already had eleven children. At eleven Tom passed the exam for entry to grammar school; the only one of that family to do so; or so it seemed. Tom was allowed to take up the scholarship (though had to do his homework on the tram to and from school). He went on to become the first Headmaster of a large secondary modern school. Only many years later was it generally known that two of his male cousins in that house, each a few years older than Tom, had also passed that exam— but had not been allowed to take up the scholarships. They were needed to go to work. The belt tightened, the possible ladder was pulled away. I still do not know exactly why only two or three years later Tom was allowed to accept the offer. Perhaps opinion in that household had broadened. Or perhaps the memory of our mother had come into play; they had thought of her as from a slightly higher class. Did that memory prompt the feeling that one of her children should not be denied a suitable education?

It is no wonder that, in the light of this dominant, enclosing lack of expectations, yet another group of dour idioms were gathered: 'One swallow doesn't make a summer', 'what's done can't be undone', 'don't tempt fate', 'better safe than sorry', 'leave well alone', 'look before you leap', 'cut your coat according to your cloth', 'don't get above yourself', and so, drearily, on. Somewhere here belongs that ambiguously foreboding: 'A new broom sweeps clean'. It can be interpreted straightforwardly and almost cheerfully, in favour of the effectiveness of new brooms. It can be heard more sombrely and unexpectantly, about, say, a new boss who tries to make a good impression by 'sweeping clean', but who may confidently be expected soon to be like all his forerunners, as the bristles wear out—sloppy, inefficient. self-regarding.

There were, of course, a lot of handy phrases to express admiration for one who has in spite of everything 'got on', especially by being clever, 'bright'. That belonged to another, more traditionally-to-be-respected world. There were many other sayings about those who had got on through sharp practice, especially if that involved cheating others of their own kind, having always 'an eye on the main chance', 'taking care of number one', 'feathering his own nest', 'making sure he saves his own bacon'. Yet after all, might be added, 'It's "every man's for himself" in the long run'; and no matter how much money a man may make, it's often 'clogs to clogs in three generations'. That adage had special comforting force in those streets, like a delayed prize for them; retribution upon the smart arse. In America they amended it to 'from shirt-sleeves to shirt-sleeves in three generations', Lancashire clogs not having been heard there.

Caution

Unexpectancy breeds excessive caution, being careful not to reach too far out in case you miss, lose your footing, and forfeit even what little you have. That is one thick root of working-class caution, a kind of super-prudence and a touch of fearfulness. It can also be fed by cannyness, shrewdness, even low cunning, biting every proferred coin at least twice. One is daily driven in that direction by the facts of life, by constant lines drawn short, by the realisation that though you may have little there are usually some—many—who would like to con you out of it. You may or may not be cautious by nature; nurture will see to it that you develop at least some degree of caution, or else you will suffer. The 'lessons of life' can be hard, unremitting, unforgiving. It is no use being 'wise after the event'. 'Don't tempt fate'. Remember that 'a fool and his money are soon parted', especially if you have occasionally 'more money than sense' (by winning something on the Pools, perhaps). The line seems endless.

'Leave well alone', 'look before you leap', 'there's many a slip', 'don't count your chickens before they're hatched', 'if wishes were horses', 'prevention is better than cure', 'anything for a quiet life', 'don't buy a pig in a poke', ' it's no use shutting the stable door after the horse has bolted' (again, not many chickens, pigs or horses around Hunslet but the images had not faded in the mind), 'don't put all your eggs in one basket', 'don't bite off more than you can chew', 'don't be always chopping and changing', 'don't touch that for love or money'—or, 'for all the tea in China'. Probably this explains why some prosperous professionals, long away from their working-class origins, can still habitually and momentarily hesitate to buy the first round or be the first to reach for the restaurant bill. Relaxed generosity is hard to acquire.

A recent, extreme, cautionary example from a 'sink' estate. A young husband and father, often in debt, was declared redundant and given a lump sum as severance payment; more than he had ever had at one time. With it, he bought a fourth-hand car and said he meant to learn to drive. He forgot about that and the car lay in front of the house until it was taken apart by the local lads. He had a phone installed since he had 'always fancied one'. He was pleased to let the neighbours have free use of it; until BT removed it after his debts had become high and there seemed no sign of payment. Soon, all the money was gone, and he still owed as much as ever, or more. That was self-destruction, unaided by the local conmen.

Time to take breath before starting again on the litany of caution, protectiveness, suspicion: 'Don't cross that bridge till you come to it,' 'save your breath to cool your broth', 'take care you don't get the mucky end of the stick', 'don't stick your nose out too soon', 'once bitten, twice shy', 'fine words butter no parsnips' (that's for the local con-men especially), 'believe nothing of what you hear and only half of what you see' (an interesting distinction by which you are urged to trust your own eyesight more than the tempting words of others—sounds reasonable), 'the leopard doesn't change his spots' (from Jeremiah), 'a bad penny always turns up again' (and the penny itself, we saw earlier, often turns up in these admonitions), 'pigs might fly'. If you do make some money, 'don't let it burn a hole in your pocket', 'more haste, less speed', 'the proof of the pudding is in the eating'. Warnings against over-reaching range from the fairly cheerful to the gloomy: 'A bird in the hand is worth two in the bush', 'don't try to run before you can walk', and the sombre: 'more wants more'.

There are many more of these several varieties of caution, but only a few extra will be enough, such as: 'forewarned is forearmed' and 'a stitch in time'. Like the image of a penny, the sense of the movement of time pops up regularly here and no doubt will do so elsewhere: 'One step at a time', 'time is a great healer', 'it's early days yet', 'a stitch in time saves nine', 'time will tell', 'time can work wonders'. Patience is buttressed by confidence in letting matters have time to work themselves out.

Inevitably, rural epigrams have a favoured place. Some things may take 'donkey's. years' to come to fruition, or to 'come home to roost'; perhaps 'till the cows come home'; 'a miss is as good as a mile', 'it's a long lane that has no turning', 'you can't have it both ways' (sometimes you can, as many exploiters large and small know well), and a particularly silly/sententious one: 'you can't have your cake and eat it' (if you've eaten it you still have it—in your stomach, which is presumably what you intended, so you can hardly grumble; and to leave it uneaten would be pointless. Perhaps that solemn saw is meant to be advice to a thoughtless spendthrift), 'you can have too much of a good thing' (ugh, very sour, tight-lipped, illiberal). 'Chance would be a fine thing' seems a fair riposte to this; and we'll ourselves decide after that whether we have had too much; 'all good things come to an end' (so they do and perhaps that's often 'all to the good'), 'a watched pot never boils'. How obvious and obviously mistaken are some of these; as empty as some of today's overused banalities, such as: 'I'll give you a bell', 'I was gutted' and 'I've been to hell and back' (the two last being cant expressions much used to justify excessive claims for damages after an accident or unfavourable treatment).

So they march on: 'Rome wasn't built in a day', 'there's a time and place for everything' (True, but that depends on who is deciding). 'Many a slip betwixt cup and lip', 'don't walk before you can run', 'let sleeping dogs lie', 'there's no smoke without fire' (that is a particularly nasty and prejudicial example; there can be almost clean smoke with no or very little fire; much depends on the source); 'bad news travels fast' (true—especially via the street gossips).

Finally, two particularly odd ones: 'Laughter before breakfast, tears before supper' (sounds like something from a most Calvinistic household; is there a necessarily unhappy connection between a cheerful morning and a miserable, penalty-paying evening?). Then, a flat dire warning: 'For want of a nail the shoe was lost / For want of a shoe the horse was lost / For want of a horse the rider was lost'. I heard that more than once in the back-to-back terraces of Leeds, as always with no sense of irrelevance or archaism.

Robust and Often Cheerful Resistances

So far a lot of weight here—perhaps too much—has been put on the more dour and sometimes sour aspects of older working-class attitudes, as those were expressed in favourite idioms. It is time to redress the balance, to look at more robust reactions, at bloody-minded resistances, more positive expressions of 'keeping your end up', refusals to accept unexpectancy, finding individual determination. These are all parts of the refusal to be 'looked down upon', the assertion of self-respect, of not being willing to be 'beholden' to anyone, not to 'bow and scrape'. They work against that unhorizoned, unperspectived unexpectancy which encouraged a lack of initiative in most people, and still does in too many.

Too much in their lives said: best to stay in your place; stick within your group, with your neighbours, your mates ('mates' is now exceptionally widely and loosely used outside its older use by men working together in a group or gang. Hold a door open for someone you have never met and you are likely to hear 'Thanks, mate'). The acceptance that you would do well to stick with your mates can still be true, but was never the whole truth. It defines limits too hopelessly. It recalls and applies with new force Granville-Barker's haunting phrase about professional disgrace. That, too, fits the panorama of pre-war working-class life: 'It's the waste, the waste that I resent'; the waste of talent, of potential, of possibilities. The common if unspoken assumption among many people, better-endowed from birth, that on the whole the less-gifted among us sink, *have* already sunk, to the bottom and should be content there, is a comforting myth; nurture here counts for far more than nature. Many quite ungifted people born into the middle and upper classes stay where they are, buoyed-up by the safety-net resources of their groups. G. B. Shaw advised us not to forget that though few rise, some also fall. True, but they are even fewer than the risers.

Yet, down there, are also many expressions of optimism, a surprisingly large range of especially liked sayings: 'It's never too late to mend', 'you've got to look on the bright side', the relentlessly optimistic 'every cloud has a silver lining', 'it's a long lane that has no turning' and 'it's an ill wind that blows no one any good', 'better to travel hopefully than to arrive' (where's the opposition there? Even hopeful travel that doesn't end at its chosen destination would be pointless), 'there's plenty more fish in the sea (or) where that came from' (useful for cheering up a jilted lover of either sex), 'wonders will never cease' (though that is usually spoken rather ironically; the 'wonder' may be some quite small surprise, a gift or an unexpected and uncharacteristically kind act, a thoughtfulness).

Some unexpected and unwanted changes prove beneficial, perhaps prompt new starts, even if they are brought about by your getting the sack and being forced to look elsewhere; that may be 'a blessing in disguise'; after all, a change can be 'as good as a rest'. I'm not going simply to sit around waiting for when 'my ship comes in', though I'm glad that 'God tempers the wind to the shorn lamb', and I always try to remember: 'laugh and the world laughs with you / weep and you weep alone'. 'You never know what you can do 'til you try', 'burn your boats' and take the risk, be ready to 'sink or swim'.

This more positive line proves to be as long as that which contains those dozens of merely-putting-up-with-things phrases, or even longer: 'In for a penny, in for a pound', 'strike while the iron is hot'; so you've had a set-back, but that's 'not the end of the world'. Don't let yourself 'go to the dogs' (that usually refers to 'going downhill' by spending too much money in betting on greyhound racing; I prefer my own error in interpretation: that it means 'going downhill' until you look like an unkempt mongrel), and don't 'rest on your laurels' if you've just managed to get some laurels to rest on, 'don't cry before you're hurt', 'where there's a will there's a way', 'we'll cross that bridge when we come to it', 'it's a poor heart that never rejoices'. When some change hits the family, for good or ill, the epigrams swirl out and around like confetti: 'time heals all wounds', 'you can't win them all', 'worse things happen at sea', 'God helps those who help themselves', 'the best things in life are free', 'don't meet trouble half-way', 'sufficient to the day is the evil thereof'' (sometimes biblical memories are drawn on more than usual—especially when resisting adversity; biblical cheerfulness is less common).

The usual old images from the country come a close second here. If some of Hunslet's inhabitants tried to 'save for a rainy day', it wasn't usually prompted by the fact that rain would spoil any day's work—unless they were, say, builders in the open air—as it had affected for centuries agricultural workers who were 'rained off' and probably not paid for such days. Yet that image had a more than usual hold, perhaps because it was so difficult 'to live up to', to bring about by self-discipline.

That brings to mind a comic incident. My wife, who comes from the Cheshire/Lancashire borders, will sometimes say on a particularly rainy day: 'Ah well, it's fine weather for ducks'. Simple wry irony. Setting out from an Austrian *pension* on such a day, the family 'all dressed up' against the elements, we met the proprietor at the door, complaining about the weather. My wife produced her 'ducks' image, one of the many. The proprietor looked mystified. Why on earth was this English lady saying something obvious but not in any way relevant to us all, about 'ducks'? The irony escaped her; that oblique, dry, inconsequential, Lewis Carrollish manner of speech was alien. Quirky duck references are common in English literature, for example, in *The Old Curiosity Shop*.

Ducks were not common in Stalybridge any more than were horses, but that didn't stop anyone from using duck and horse epigrams on any possible occasion. Cats were ubiquitous, but few were almost killed by care; many were more likely to be killed by eating muck they picked up in the street or by being run over. There was only a small amount of—dirty—grass under your feet which you were advised not to let grow further, and no hay at all for you to make while the sun shone. You were not often tempted to try to kill two birds with one stone, stones being scarce and house-sparrrows nimble.

The dance of historic cheering-up idioms went on nimbly, too, though, through some sentences uttered occasionally even by the most hopelessly poverty-stricken. You were, as might need be, ready 'to fight tooth and nail', to 'do or die', to 'stick to your guns' (memories of Kipling's Tommies), to 'move Heaven and Earth' towards a goal (though most could not be said to have a goal). You tried to 'make the best of a bad job', to 'improve the shining hour'. You might just intone 'nothing ventured, nothing gained' and 'where there's a will there's a way'—whilst always being careful 'not to have too many irons in the fire'. Still, you could comfort yourself with the thought that 'many a mickle makes a muckle'.

The ballet continued. That many of those tags contradict each other is, we saw much earlier, beside the point; they often sound like unimpeachable truths but are really forms of verbal instant poultice, reassuring utterances for each occasion and, once uttered, put aside in the memory bin until needed again.

The not undeniable but often heartening ones are comforting: 'No news is good news', 'It wouldn't do for us all to have long faces', 'every little helps', 'good health is better than wealth' and its variant: 'you can put up with anything so long as you have your health', 'he who hesitates is lost', 'we live and learn', 'God helps those who help themselves' (I expect that's an encouragement to 'put your shoulder to the wheel' but was early struck by the thought of a burglar in a cartoon muttering it to himself as he made off with the bag labelled 'Swag'); 'Yer've got to laugh, 'aven't yer', when some not very serious mishap strikes, was partnered by: 'you've got to see the funny side of things'. That repeated wartime saying of the charwoman, Mona Lott, in ITMA on the radio, uttered entirely lugubriously: 'It's being so cheerful that keeps me going', instantly and comically drew on an old root. So, incidentally, did Wilfred Pickles' equally repetitive cheerfulness at that time: 'Go on. 'Ave a go!' Having a go, like having a flutter, is one of the few totally free acts.

So: 'don't meet trouble half-way' but, when especially hard-up, observe: 'Ah well, there's corn in Egypt' (Genesis: the instruction to Joseph to 'get moving'); an injunction for the self-justifyingly shiftless. On the other hand, be careful, you might 'Go further and fare worse'. And remember that 'a bird in the hand…' You may find that your new experiences are 'nothing to write home about' (said so as to 'play down' what the writer might think good news, and probably said by recipients who have rarely had occasion to write home with good news or bad throughout their lives); and after all remember that 'everything comes to him who waits'. Linked to those are the depressingly static ones, especially through the manner in which they are usually uttered: 'There's no ways like the old ways' and 'old habits die hard'. Sometimes a hearer can share those, but not when they are used to justify inaction, listlessness, the refusal ever to adapt to change.

The 'writing home' adage recalls a very few others which seem against the terms of working-class life. We very often said that something—some decision to act—was 'as safe as houses'. That seems more like a lower-middle-class or middle-class expression; you put your money into buying a house or even houses (as an investment) rather than into a bank account, because you knew that 'bricks and mortar' generally appreciated in value, were translatable capital. But almost all the people who easily used that phrase were renting their homes without hope of ever buying them, of getting together enough money to put down a deposit towards a mortgage. They knew that, but, laconically, enjoyed the excessive assumption—if they thought of it.

One could go on. And on. But let this chapter end with a few mixed sayings that are intriguing even if not always easy to understand: 'It's as cheap sitting as standing'. Not in a football ground, it isn't. So where, then? In church? At a crematorium? In a tram or bus? It is certainly used to encourage someone, say, a wife or a friend, to join you in taking available seats. But that is a limited application; surely it has an inverted ironic meaning?

'You could have knocked me down with a feather'. Simple, overused, but exact and much loved by comedians: 'Eh, missus, when she said that you could have knocked me down with a feather'.

A depressed one for a change: 'Yer look like someone that's lost a shilling and found sixpence'. And three to cheer us up: another dog one, 'every dog has his day ', which offers hope to all underdogs but, apart from all else, always reminds me of once seeing a mongrel coming delightedly upon a bitch in heat down our street; but that's too literal; true, though. Then, the firm optimism of 'it's a poor heart that never rejoices' and the more down to earth assurance of 'when one door shuts another opens'. All in all, the weight seems to come down on the hopeful side.

Yes, of course, many of these, probably most, were used across society. But, used as often and with the same weight as by working-class people? On this evidence that seems very unlikely. No other group is likely to have had and regularly to have been led to use so many apophthegms about the condition of being poor, to have been led to adopt and adapt so many other idioms so as to reflect their condition. For them, the frequency and stress in the use of this wide range of idioms was definitive. Being poor bore on many of them heavily, all the time. They had to have images for all aspects of it. No doubt today's prosperous 'working class' has no need to call on many of them; the underclass still does.

Such a cluster of uses can have a double role. They reflect the uniqueness of working-class experience, and in doing so they draw on the language of a larger culture, on something of a common culture, national and even international, through both space and time. Though many are used widely, few are used in the same way by different groups; they are part of a different mix, composition, social and personal world.

*   *   *

We should be able to assess better which images are likely to remain and which to disappear after looking more closely at different parts of current 'working-class' experience. Changes in the sense of neighbourliness, as housing becomes less cramped, more dispersed, often more vertical than horizontal; the considerable changes across classes in the roles played by women, whether at home or, more importantly, as wage-earners; general increases in freely available money; and changes in the nature of work and work relationships, as globalization increases: these are four factors which will cause some idioms to fall into disuse. It will be interesting to hear what new and more relevant idioms succeed them and why; how the new phrases mirror those social changes or indicate others less obvious at present. Many will; but whether they will have the staying-power of those they have succeeded will be another interesting question.

3

Family and Neighbourhood (I)

Home, home to my woman, where the fire's lit
These still chilly mid-May evenings.
—Tony Harrison, 'V'

'No Place Like Home'

Most writing about earlier—say, pre-1960—working-class life, is likely to be received suspiciously by some readers, especially if a writer recalls any of its compensations. George Orwell was accused of an old-Etonian's sentimental patronage for that passage in *The Road to Wigan Pier* on the comely decencies of some working-class interiors. A quarter of a century later my description of some similar homes (one shouldn't really have to keep inserting that qualifying 'some') in pre-war Leeds drew the same accusations. Certain writers, especially those also from working-class backgrounds and who have strong political convictions, react against any description which does not stress the politically active nature of most—as they like to insist—of the working class, yet does mentions some of those warmer domestic qualities. In turn, writers from the middle class may react as though a powerful and comforting myth has been damaged.

That the majority of working-class men were not active politically is not the only amendment such writers do not wish to accept; they do not like to hear that many workmen returned and return tired, but gladly, to their homes after work. That many wives also have settled for that way of going on can suggest to such critics that they were drudges or doormats, victims; and their husbands culpably inert. As is the way with the journals of opinion, those criticisms have entered the closed circuit of received judgments and are passed from mouth to mouth, some by people who know almost nothing of those earlier households and may not even have read Orwell's notorious passage; they are content to dismiss or denigrate it at second-hand. Some of those who have been brought up in politically active working-class homes dismiss it at first-hand, and out-of-hand.

Working-class home life could be, then, surprisingly warm and kindly. It could also be unhappy, torn with the sense of shortage and failure (as ours was); it could be brutal, beer-bespattered, foul-mouthed. Again, that should not need saying; it is obvious, and something like it could be said about a range of middle-class or, perhaps, upper-class homes.

And so, many working-class homes managed, in spite of privations, low expectations and often unappetising working conditions, to become quiet and affectionate oases. If some people find this hard to accept from discursive writers perhaps they will lend a more attentive ear to a poet. Tony Harrison's loving depiction of his Leeds working-class home, of the deep and lasting affection between his parents and the warmth which enveloped the children, rings true and is captured in touches that should move even a sceptical outsider, especially the lines in 'Long Distance' on his father's unconsolable grief on his wife's death:

> 'Though my mother was already two years dead
> Dad kept her slippers warming by the gas,
> put water bottles her side of the bed
> and still went to renew her transport pass.'

He was unremittingly miserable; those touches—the slippers, the water bottles, the transport pass—could have been regarded as slightly 'cracked' by the neighbours (he hid any they might see), but they established a small continuing connection.

Hence that all-embracing sense of the home, as against if not the hostility then the unfriendliness of much in the world outside, made 'hearth and home' essential but not unique to working-class culture. It is especially striking in working-class homes because there, as has already been said but bears repeating, so much might seem to work against it; there, it is a positive and strong bulwark. In an over-stressed, cartoon-like manner the television programme, *The Royles,* caught some of that, made funnier because the main lines were too broadly insistent; that's the way television propels re-creations, so that they fit its own nature. But the congenital clustering, like that of nesting creatures, is broadly true.

So it can be in some, perhaps many, other cultures; and other classes. Auden, that sadly unrooted man, praised the uniquely strong

English talent for creating an agreeable family life. I do not imagine he had Orwell's working class in mind but, rather, his own professional middle class. The Auden family itself? Perhaps. Just as likely, though, he was recalling the families of his circle of staunch friends. Yet his claim for English supremacy here is not easily borne out.

In Naples during the war one of our 'gunners' (privates), a working-class cockney, formed an unlikely friendship with a singer from the San Carlo Opera Company. That started by his going round to the stage-door to express his admiration; he wasn't shy. She, too, was working class, from the back-streets of the city (like the effective talent-scouts for budding rugby league players in the crammed streets of Northern towns, the Naples Opera had a clever eye for potentially fine voices in its even more crowded slums). The gunner was soon invited home, to the main Sunday meal, a feast buttressed by pasta in the way that many English working-class Sunday dinners are buttressed, and not only in the North, by Yorkshire pudding. He told me about this similarity himself, being struck by the same warmth, talkativeness, and general contentment as at their Sunday dinners back home.

'No place like home' (that has come all the way from Hesiod's *Works and Days*); 'East West, Home's best': poker-work mottoes of that kind would be found in many of our interiors, almost as often as the rank aspidistra. That unattractive and dull Asian plant, much loved by the Victorian middle class, had spread like ground elder into most working-class homes. One did not often see small, brownish flowers; perhaps our polluted atmosphere had made most plants sterile. It was admired rather than liked. Perhaps its capacity for sturdy life against all the odds appealed to something in working-class people, as a spirit which thrived, however unpromising its surroundings. Hence Gracie Fields's raucous song of triumph about *The Biggest Aspidistra in the World*.

To return to the poker-work injunctions hung on many walls. Typically, they eulogised not only the Home but also Home-with-Religion, as in 'May God Guard this House'. D. H. Lawrence recalled them ironically when in *Sons and Lovers,* at the height of a family 'row', the older boy William looks up and reads out just such a prayer hanging on the wall: *God Bless our Home.*

So, as we have already seen from another angle: family first, your 'own flesh and blood', 'your nearest and dearest'; for 'blood is thicker than water'. Then the concentric circles of others usually from the streets around, parents (grandma and grandad), married sisters and brothers, in-laws, the occasional close friend of your own generation, neighbours; plus, in time, the kids' friends. This was the neighbourhood, the core of your life outside, with its compass centred in the extended family of three generations. That phrase—'community'—so widely over-used and wrongly used nowadays: 'in this close-knit community there is deep shock today that [something awful has happened]..., etc'.—that sort of language could apply then in many areas; it applies less today.

The readiness to move even a few streets away was not to be taken for granted. A young man—this was as late as the eighties, in middle England—brought up in the lower middle class, had left grammar school and was well started on a promising career. He married a girl who would be regarded as respectable working class, an assistant in a 'good' shop in town. After a few years the man's firm sent him, an indication that they thought well of his work, to their headquarters on the South Coast. By then they had two young children. His wife dug in with considerable force; she refused to move. The old staunch saying by diplomatic wives about their own tasks on relocation: 'Pay, pack and follow', would have been not only alien but entirely unacceptable to her. She produced an almost gnomic final utterance: 'But we live in Newark. We're Newark people'. Clearly, she expected him to refuse the offer and find another job in Newark; no ladder of ambition for her, no vertical climb. The husband went down South, coming home at weekends to a wife more and more engrossed in the two girls and Newark. Gradually the ties weakened. He found another woman who moved with him as work required. Eventually there was a divorce. The former wife lived on in Newark with her daughters. Her father came round regularly and happily—'religiously', neighbours might have said—to do whatever handiwork she needed about the house; Newark people, and those of many another similar town, are like that, put that sort of belonging first. The girl remarried, to a carpenter, a Newark carpenter, who did not think of moving from the town.

That favourite closure quoted above, in talk about moves outside the area: 'East West, home's best', was by many taken as an unassailable truth, like 'absence makes the heart grow fonder'. No wonder the parable of the Prodigal Son was such a favourite in the chapels; it rang true for both the loss and the welcome return after no matter how long (unless, or sometimes even if, the prodigal had 'blotted his copybook').

No wonder too that the homesickness of the Tommy as well as his resilience and 'fighting spirit'—and the loss of him felt by those back home—have been dwelt on by many writers, notably Hardy and Kipling. The music-halls, of course, rang with it, both sentimentally and belligerently. In Kipling, it went alongside the battlefield bravado of Empire building; for that, Hardy was disinclined and thought more of 'lads' lying face-down-dead in foreign fields instead of treading the earth of Dorset.

As late as the last war our Battery's gunners used still to sing, 'We all love the screw-gun', with not much provocation; it had a nice swing which went well with dull repetitive work, cleaning the guns, or boring journeys crammed in the back of trucks, long after the days of the screw-gun (which Kipling hymned). On other occasions and more often they drew on a range of cynical and often obscene songs about the army, matched with sentimentality about getting home to Blighty. The sentimental ones could be traced back to those late Victorian music-halls; the cynical and obscene were usually the work of anonymous masters; or, it was often said, of Noel Coward. That usually enclosed world, musically, easily took over *Lili Marlene*; it fitted so well that it overrode nationalism.

One member of a Stalybridge family I know had fought at Gallipoli when seventeen, having given a false age. He got out of there unscathed and never left Britain again. Until he died he was likely to intone, on suitable prompting: 'No need to leave England. England is the most beautiful country on earth'. How did he know? He was never challenged. He was wrapped in his nationality, like his French and German and Italian and Russian counterparts. Gallipoli was typically 'abroad' to him and he had hated it. That First World War was the last of a sequence which made working-class men even more chauvinistic, or at the least unshakeably parochial.

Working-class people were assumed by and large to stay with their roots, and most expected no more; 'abroad' was foreign and not to be trusted; the food rotten; and those people's ways probably no better than they should be. Yet for centuries the 'powers that be' sent those men out to fight and often die for Crown and Empire; and it did not seem to most, neither to 'Them' nor to 'Us', an extraordinarily sad fate, or even to point an ironic contrast between the neglect of the condition of the rankers at home and what was proudly and with noisy insistence expected of them when serving in the Empire.

Rankers could be their own sort of jingoists, too. But the 'salt of the earth' patronage towards 'the chaps' who went over the top in Flanders always rang nastily; better the Iron Duke, Wellington, saying bluntly that whatever effect they had on the enemy, his men scared the living daylights out of him; a very rough lot indeed, 'when it came to it'.

Jingoism, chauvinism, nationalism, patriotism...the line grows slightly acceptable as you move along it. Some people will interpret the last word decently, but they are fairly rare in all classes.

If a relative, a son let us say, took off, left home, and kept only intermittently in touch until eventually he was not in touch at all, the sadness lasted. Absence didn't always make the heart grow fonder, especially in the absentee, it seemed. There were usually one or two of those from each street and the routine response to enquirers was, 'Ah well, it's out of sight, out of mind, yer know'...haven't heard nor seen hide nor hair of him for months now '. A smaller number of those might eventually turn out to be 'black sheep"; chapel-bible memories again there. Less dramatic but still very painful sometimes, an attentive son might eventually bring home a girl who 'had airs' and embarrassed the family. *Sons and Lovers* again, and the excruciating scene when William brings home his girl friend from down South:

> 'Thank you so much', said the girl. [that 'so much', which runs from the lower middle class to the middle class, is particularly silly and sterile. Perhaps it is a favoured variant of 'thank you very much', though that is at least vaguely measured. 'Thank you so much' prompts the response 'How much'? A vague genteel wave.] 'Thank you so much,' said the girl, seating herself in the collier's arm-chair, the place of honour.... The young lady did not realise them as people; they were creatures to her for the present. William winced. In such a household, in Streatham, Miss Western would have been a lady condescending to her inferiors. These people were, to her, certainly clownish—in short, the working-classes. How was she to adjust herself?

Distressing. Miss Western was, of course, not middle class but insecure lower middle class, hanging on in there by her aspirated, polished, verbal fingernails.

Wars—and Changes in Outlook

Wars have had a more important, socially seismic effect on attitudes to travel than is always realised. Our father served in the Boer War and, later, since he was a regular soldier, Malta was one of his postings; we do not know of any others. He came back and took up his trade again, until the next war, the First World War, in which the bulk of army servicemen went to France and suffered the horrors of the trenches. If they were lucky they came back to their home-towns; and few after that felt inclined to leave England again. J. B. Priestley's reminiscences of the infantrymen in the *Bradford Pals* before, during and after, their long time in the trenches, are intensely moving in their closeness, their Englishness, their comradeship, their parochialness and indeed their insularity. There are no good grounds for thinking that the German private soldiers were different. My father-in-law was much the same. Sent home wounded from his Lancashire infantry regiment he never ventured abroad again, nor wished to. Nowhere better than England. He did not actually say that—he was not jingoistic—but it was probably quietly there, as one of his deeper roots.

By contrast the last war was much more a war of movement, across huge distances—Southern Europe, the Eastern Mediterranean, North Africa, the Indian sub-continent, the expanses of Asia, the Antipodes. All branches of the armed forces became used to being moved over these distances, sometimes very rapidly, increasingly by air. How far this went into the psyches of most is hard even to guess, but it seems likely to have to a certain extent opened some minds to the sense of space far beyond those muddy wastes of Flanders which were all of 'abroad' so many of their fathers knew, and beyond their own constricted home-and-work areas.

Not many years after all that was over, roughly in the middle-sixties, when we were pulling out of most post-war deprivations, air travel became cheaply available. So that by now millions, including the children and grandchildren of the 1930s working class, are likely, so long as the husband is in fairly well-paid work (or if the wife works then that will often compose the annual nest-egg for a fortnight on the Costa Brava and the like) to take a family holiday abroad each year. The statistics alone are formidable.

How far does all this contribute towards cultural change, greater cultural understanding, less chauvinism, among all those millions? The influence is probably slight. Most of us move from home, in sealed cigar-shaped containers, and land to unaccustomed regular sunshine and mowed sand, but usually expect and get our own English food, starting with one kind of 'fry-up' or another, and chips. Chips with everything. Other cultural shifts are likely to be small and slow. Perhaps more in the next generation, backpacking across the world, often in a gap-year or soon after becoming the first graduates in their families, will cause changes, there as elsewhere.

When the time is ripe, it will be fascinating to assess the ways in which that first large group may have changed the more routinely accepted and deeply bedded attitudes of their parents. We do not seem to know much about that octopoid process of cultural change through unconscious filtration, of how new ideas move slowly down from the intellectuals through the 'gatekeepers' of opinion of several kinds, who let some things through and others not, and at last into everyday talk and everyday opinions. But is that question itself too intellectually put? Are ideas, attitudes, as much changed by horizontal extension, spreading like a new colour of ink outwards from the talk of local, at-hand, opinion formers, often at the place of work, by some who may themselves read little except the popular press, a process which will have its effects but not always as a straight and unquestioned transference. People can and often do think for themselves, though one wouldn't guess that from the way journalists and politicians harangue them.

Meanwhile, as the popular language still shows, the hold of home, of the local district, and the mild suspicion of most things foreign (and of some other parts of these islands), remain, not greatly altered.

The Main Characters

Wives and Mothers

> As a child I am always conscious and always guilty—that I love my mother more than my father. I am happier with her rather than with him, feel easier alone in her company, whereas with him I am awkward and over-talkative and not the kind of boy (modest, unassuming and unpretentious) that I feel he wants me to be and has been himself.
>
> —Telling Tales

Alan Bennett's quiet confession comes in well there. It would have been easier to explain away if his father had been brutal, a bad husband, a boozer, something like that. He was none of those things. The boy's links to his mother went much deeper, were founded in no such obvious alienations.

The central character in a typical working-class home is overwhelmingly the wife and mother. The discussion of her roles is another minefield or field of fire from which no writer is likely to emerge

unscathed. Much emotional energy is invested in different and conflicting opinions.

My own opinion is that those who put the woman at the very
heart of family life are more often right than their opponents.
Patmore's *Angel in the House* sounds saccharine to almost all of us
today, but try to read it 'straight' and you find an honest celebration,
honestly faced.

Of course, there are bad mothers, neglectful mothers; there are
also mothers who are bad wives; and some are both at once. There
are good husbands and devoted fathers.

But more women than men hold families and homes together;
that is an assertion which can't easily be proved scientifically except
in limited ways, but observation compellingly suggests it. It can be
guessed at from the way the most horrible of grown men—gang-
sters from London's East End, say—so often refer sentimentally
to their mothers when they can hardly offer residual good feeling to anyone else, probably including their fathers and often
their wives. It can be seen every day throughout our lives if we
wish to observe it. It begins in a fact of nature. It runs through
literature of all ages. You will not find much in Graham Greene, but
you will in D. H. Lawrence. Read only that hauntingly reminiscent
poem, 'Piano':

> Softly, in the dusk, a woman is singing to me
> Taking me back down the vista of years, till I see
> A child sitting under the piano, in the boom of the
> tingling strings
> And pressing the small poised feet, of a mother who
> smiles as she sings.
>
> In spite of myself, the insidious mastery of song
> Betrays me back, till the heart of me weeps to belong
> To the old Sunday evenings at home...

—which was on many other occasions a brutal home. Or one can
recall those lines of Tony Harrison quoted earlier. They bear men-
tioning again—these plain truths—because today, as with arguments
about the good atmosphere in many working-class homes, some
people back away from the thought of such 'rightness', 'being in
the truth', and see the claim as rather a form of patronage, a reducing of the independent role and spirit of women. One needs finer
tools than that to see into the real strength and power of most women
in the home, especially in their relations with men who may from

the outside seem, are allowed to seem, and seem to themselves, the dominant partner in each pair.

This need not at all be by the nightly tribune of the marital bed; it is much more subtle than that, much more an elaborate subterranean play of different kinds of emotional and moral strength, much more a matter of invisible, unacknowledged but powerful accommodatings. Listen, if you have the opportunity, to a discussion between husband and wife about, say, whether the bright child, girl or boy, shall take up the opportunity for higher education and so remain not a contributor to the family purse, and perhaps risk moving out from the family setting altogether, or on whether a certain boy-friend is suitable for a steady relationship with a daughter.

'An Englishman's home is his castle' is an inadequate epigram which was hardly heard roundabout us, except very occasionally from a boastful drunk. There is an irony there. Sir Edward Coke in the 17th century ruled that if you shut yourself up no bailiff can break through, arrest or take goods. Apparently that still holds though no one in Hunslet had seemed to have heard of it. We thought the bailiff's right of entry absolute.

One heard much more often: 'a woman's work is never done' and that was mainly from women who uttered it slightly ruefully but not in a kicking-against-the-pricks manner. 'No rest for the wicked' joined that wry-but-largely-cheerful lexicon. Similarly 'a woman's place is in the home' was uttered long before it became usual for women to go out to work, and was not normally an admission of submission. At that time it was often said by a woman who thought a neighbour was being selfish by going out to work unnecessarily and so risking not fulfilling her responsibilities to her husband and, even more, her children, at an age when they did need her more than they needed their father, who was anyway out at his work all day, and who was admittedly the main and apparently irreplaceable pivot of the home, financially.

Since so many women do go out to work nowadays it may be assumed that many more men help about the house. This does seem to have spread in the middle and lower middle classes; in working-class homes the record is patchy, the spread downwards slow. A lot of men seem unable to get into their heads the need for sharing household chores now as both may come home tired; such sharing seems against nature to them, and to some women. Similarly, at rock bottom (or perhaps not so deep down) one may still hear men in a pub saying that if a girl becomes pregnant through them, then 'It's her fucking look-out'; not much hope of 'safe sex' there.

Husband and Father

So, insofar as one can generalise, the husband and father was more often than not psychologically the secondary partner in these relationships. Yet in looking at him there appears a contradiction greater than any which involves the wife. As the main or probably only breadwinner, the one who went out to work early and came back 'dog-tired,' he could expect, if not to be 'waited on hand and foot', then certainly to be given very sympathetic attention, understandably at that time. 'The way to a man's heart [being] through his stomach', his evening meal would be put on the table within minutes of his coming through the door, no washing-up required of him, his particular place near the fire taken for granted. This was likely to be accorded both to husbands who in many ways 'were good about the house' and to selfish husbands who took the excuse of 'dog-tiredness' as a justification for 'not ever doing a hand's turn', who would not 'stir their stumps' even when the wife was 'up to her eyes in work', not feeling very well, or even was pregnant. One Hunslet man I knew was so typical of all those assumptions and practices that one felt that he ought himself, so long as his wife was protected, be preserved as an 'icon'.

Again at a guess, in almost all back-to-back streets there were more 'good husbands' than bad; but the bad made more noise and attracted more attention. Occasionally, a fight developed outside a house or on a bit of spare land, perhaps because of suspected adultery, but those were rare. Nowadays, one hears much more, especially in lower-middle-class and middle-class circles, of husbands or wives having affairs. Their work no doubt can provide more temptations since the sexes are likely to be mixed there and the women more often younger than the men, and more often and until quite recently, in less senior positions.

Working-class men in heavy industry before the war occupied an almost totally male environment, a daily life with their mates—except when they went through their own front doors in the evening. And the pubs were chiefly for men who, especially on weekdays (though probably 'with the wife' at weekends), went there alone for a pint after the evening meal. So they were at most times predominantly places for male talk in the saloon bar, not often areas for sexual dalliance.

On the other hand, there were times when the wife did not want him 'under her feet', 'in the way'. There is a fine comic passage in Lawrence's *The Rainbow* after a young couple have had a rapturous few days of honeymoon alone in their cottage, totally absorbed physically, discovering each other's bodies and capacities for passion. Then it is over; the young wife gets out of bed, rolls up her sleeves and starts to put the place in order, to 'bottom it' in preparations for visitors. The husband gets in her way, is a bit of a nuisance; she wants him outside. He is uncomprehending and feels cast out. That rings true:

> She rose to a real outburst of homework, turning him away as she shoved the furniture aside to her broom. He stood hanging miserably near. He wanted her back.

It seems slightly odd that the word 'hubby', which can sound rather comical on first hearing, can also suggest a long, affectionate and cosy relationship. It was more commonly heard among lower-middle-class wives than among working-class. It carries, implies, much of the settled togetherness of many secure lower-middle-class marriages, perhaps never threatened by infidelity or unemployment, and hints at one of the more attractive characteristics of that maligned group. Perhaps 'hubby' was felt to be a smug word of the lower middle classes, rather soft and coy to working-class ears. It is probably in the upper class's group of silly words, such as 'toilet', which are used lower down. One hardly ever heard it in Hunslet. 'Husband'—and a few more idiomatic words—were preferred there, and occasionally slightly waggish labels such as 'my old man'.

Perhaps it needs to be said again at the end of this section that, yes, some husbands were and are 'brutes', the most commonly applied word for a wife-beater, of whom it might also be said, rather evasively: 'E doesn't treat 'er right'. What were husband-beaters called? There were some of those. Domestic violence is not, as one woman insisted in a committee's discussion on changing social habits, 'gender-specific'—to men. In our streets, husband-beating was referred to in a rather hushed way, as though it was a peculiarly shameful thing: 'she treats him badly,' 'she knocks him about', 'he's right under her thumb'. Wife-beating was shameful too, but, to the women who were willing to mention it, husband-beating was as if against nature.

One should also add that, in spite of what to many others would seem an inevitably glum way of life, there was a good deal of laughter in those streets; funny-bones could be very near the surface, ready for tickling.

Children

Working-class children were, are, often 'spoiled', over-indulged; this should not surprise. From Victorian novels we know that such children were often exploited, sent to work early, maltreated by their employers. We also know that even then some were petted, made much of, as were some in the 'pampered' middle class.

In a household not riven by bad temper or drink, or beset by unemployment (though that was not always an exception), children tended to be 'made much of', indulged, even 'spoilt'. Chapel-going, 'respectable', families were often anxious above all not to commit that last failing. They would hardly be likely to say: 'Spare the rod and spoil the child' (that comes all the way from Proverbs XIII— 24), but an attenuated form of it lingered at the backs of their minds. They did quite often say (this dates from about 1400): 'children should be seen and not heard', especially if visitors were present; but that seemed more like a routine public display of discipline than an injunction normally to be taken seriously.

Many families all around gave their children more pocket-money 'than was good for them', let them have too much money for tooth-rotting cheap sweets, and for ice-cream whenever the van came round. One of my more severe aunts regularly condemned all this out of hand as weakness of will, 'bad upbringing'. Perhaps it was inspired by the feeling that once they were out of childhood the 'real' world would not be accommodating to them, that the boys were likely to go into dead-end work and the girls, after a few years of menial employment and a brief butterfly flight—or, perhaps more accurate—moth flight towards the light, into marriages which, well-founded or not, were unlikely to be 'beds of roses'.

They, in turn, would treat their own children in much the same way. Today this has been extended well into the 'teens', propelled by the existence of more spare money and by massive advertising campaigns which exploit the growing wish to be part of the peer-group.

Of course, some were indeed 'spoilt'. There was usually one boy in the class, even at grammar school, who was plumper than the rest, especially if his mother was widowed and they lived with grand-parents. Of him, other mothers were likely to say not simply that he was 'the apple of her eye' (sometimes and in some places seen not as the fruit but as 'the core'), but that 'she thinks the sun shines out of him' or—for the vulgar ones -'out of his bum'. Excuses abounded, especially for overeating or misbehaviour: 'he does like his food, yer know', or the flaccid 'boys will be boys', and 'like father, like son', or 'he's a chip of the old block, alright'. 'Still, you can't put an old head on young shoulders'. Or, critically, 'he's tied to her apron strings' (and 'she likes it', not simply 'puts up with it', is implied). That has made him 'mardy', a mardy-arse, spoilt from overindulgence. Even more critically, if things are going wrong: 'As the twig is bent, so is the tree inclined'. One heard that only occasionally, usually from old and still slightly countrified people; it appears in 16th-century French and in Pope. It is sober. Just as popular was the sentimental, ''e's a lovable rascal', about some young yobbo.

In spite of what is said above about girls being indulged, a boy alone in the family could be spoiled rather more easily than a girl; he was not culturally connected with household duties—with cooking, ironing, sewing—though even by some girls these might be picked up unwillingly or late, not long before marriage. Still, the mother's relationship to her daughter was usually different and in the end deeper: 'Your son's your son till he takes him a wife / Your daughter's your daughter the whole of her life' (from the 17th century). That again, like the usual emotional preeminence of the mother within the family as a whole, seems more often true than not.

That days-of-the-week rhyming-round, which begins 'Monday's child is fair of face...', was also regularly invoked, but chiefly because it runs so easily. It was not often seriously invoked as a partly foreboding prediction. A child could not make much sense of 'it's a wise child that knows it's own father', until adolescence gave it a sombre meaning way beyond the normal realities, even of those streets. It is at least four centuries old and thought to refer to the assumption of greater sexual activity in the 'Dog days'. How did we come to use it? When we did, it seemed to have no sexual implication but to bear more on the idea of inherited attitudes.

Marriage

Of all aspects of working-class life, the attitude to marriage has in the last half century undergone the most startling and unexpected change. Girls would habitually put treasured things aside, in their 'bottom drawer', against marriage. They expected to become engaged and have a ring which indicated that status. They heard often that: 'good marriages are made in heaven' (16ᵗʰ century) and, from Herrick's *Hesperides* of 1648: 'Happy the bride the sun shines upon', as they went up the aisle of the church, which most of them rarely visited at other times. All this was taken seriously.

So was the obverse, though few expected that to apply to them: 'always a bridesmaid, never a bride'; did not for years seem relevant, any more than did the likelihood of being 'on the shelf' (as contrasted with putting things in the bottom drawer), or the thought that they might 'marry in haste, repent at leisure'. There was also, for bolder ones getting over the shock of being 'chucked', the consolation that: 'there's as good fish in the sea as ever came out of it' (the last two both from the 16ᵗʰ century). That last aphorism could have several wider applications; it is more easily adaptable than most.

At the worst—this was rare—girls 'put their heads in the gas oven' because they had been jilted and were perhaps pregnant. Now that household gas is non-toxic they 'take an overdose' of whatever likely pills are handy; and there may well be fewer young women driven to that extreme, for obvious reasons.

Perhaps some major attitudes in this area have radically altered, have become, in one of the most popular current epithets, more 'robust'. Here we come upon that extraordinary change, the most remarkable change in attitudes of any kind within all classes (but most surprising within the working class): the attitude towards marriage. We do not know exactly what influences brought it about though it is easy to guess at some contributors.

The contraceptive pill was approved in the USA in 1960. That, above all other influences, almost removed the fear of pregnancy which would be present even when sheaths could be used (because many men did not like sheaths, were careless, and selfish; and not all sheaths are reliable}.

By what means did that message, about the advent of the Pill and its implications, reach working-class girls? By the arguments of feminism, percolating through to women's and girls' magazines? One friend believes that, in this, working-class girls gave an earlier lead than middle-class; and that that has done much to reduce differences between those classes' cultures. Others think the lead was taken by emancipated, 'liberated' professional women working away from home before marriage. No doubt the vastly increasing numbers of students in higher education, many of them sexually active and, from the sixties, also 'liberated', added their influence. I took a taxi in the early seventies from the railway station to a new university just outside a medium-sized town. Told the address, the driver, obviously something of a card, responded: 'Oh, so you want the state-financed brothel out on the London Road?' He could as justly have said: 'state-financed marriage—or partnership—bureau'.

Other influences almost certainly include the decline of religious belief (slowest among Roman Catholics), this itself in part a result of popularised aspects of secularism; and, perhaps above all, that relativism which then began to gallop, especially after the start of the sixties, with the rise of mass-consumerism for which relativism is an essential tap-root.

At the turn into the seventies our children, when they brought a girl- or boy-friend home, were given separate bedrooms; that was simply assumed, even though we may have thought but probably not mentioned that they were 'living together' when away from us. That changed gradually, as quietly as daylight grows lighter or darker. We were of the academic middle class, a bit slow on the uptake in this matter, but on the whole moving with changing attitudes within our social group and some others close to them. Perhaps—probably—fashionable, young, city families were ahead of us.

None of this seems as interesting, indeed as startling, as the way in which so many working-class girls decided—and soon after that their parents seemed to accept—to adopt 'partnership' rather than marriage (at least in the first few years and perhaps permanently, unless the arrival of children made them, perhaps for legal or tax reasons, decide to 'tie the knot'—in that dour phrase). To underline: this is one important result of the largest, most significant and most unexpected secular change of the twentieth century in 'developed' societies.

All those bottom-drawers, and visits to C and A for brides and bridesmaids, were cast aside as though they had not held for decades a key place in the lives of young girls. How did it come about and so quickly? It is obvious that the Pill took a weight off many girls' minds if they were having sex before marriage. But that need not have undermined the institution of marriage itself, unless it led the girls to throw aside all their inhibitions and become promiscuous; and one heard only one or two convinced doom-mongers assert that, often simply as an assumption. Perhaps it all reveals that, whatever the romantic trappings accorded to marriage, many young women saw the institution at bottom chiefly as cover, an insurance policy against the dangers of being caught short, 'getting into trouble'; and now arrived at the honest realisation that, underneath, they didn't care for the constraints which could go with marriage, the risks which could attend an untested arrangement; and decided on release from it.

Naturally, even today many marry with or without all the usual trimmings. Some have parents who would be unbearably shocked by the thought of their offspring simply 'living together' and then having 'illegitimate' children—and for that are respected or humoured. Some still see marriage as a valuable symbolic assertion of their conviction that they do wish to be together, hope to live in love, for the rest of their lives.

The daughter of a friend lived in partnership for a few years and then told her father, seriously, that she and her partner meant to go to a lawyer and sign an assertion that they wished to stay together, possess goods in common and so on, all their days. The father remarked dryly that that, by and large, was what used to be called marriage and could be effected more easily and cheaply at a Registry Office. The suggestion was not taken up; in that instance something more was perhaps being resisted.

Among partners in the housing estate just over the road, there is probably little explicitly ideological thinking. Yet those in partnership seem nowadays almost equal in numbers to the married. Among old customs, marriage above all is widely regarded as out-of-date. The compacts then made are usually serious, not simply rain-cheques on possible second and third tries, but always renegotiable. That is not language most would use. Yet underneath there is a sense of greater freedom, in particular freedom to try something in good faith but to know that, if things don't 'work out', you will not still be bound for life. That seems understandable; indeed, reasonable, but is still an astonishing change.

That and other changes noted here are sure to reduce some common idioms in use; but slowly, as always. The conscious sense of radical changes in the terms of life comes gradually to virtually all of us; yet modern idioms are already all around us. Some may stay for a while and take the place of the older ones. But they, too, will be pushed aside as new inventions come along. The reaction to hectic pressure to 'change for change's sake' alone and simple emotional attachment will slow the death process of older adages. Those clas-

sic sayings will only give way when some others speak more powerfully to our fundamental conditions of life. We have seen that many,
perhaps most, of them have already lasted for centuries; they will
not soon or easily be displaced, especially in moments of crisis, and
are never likely altogether to go away, even in the prosperous West.

*   *   *

Most of what is said at the very end of the preceding chapter also
applies here, especially about the changed role of women. It is worth
repeating though, as was asserted, that some men seem able to act as
though nothing has changed, that some women will take on new
responsibilities but continue to carry all the old ones; and some
women will accept the men's assumptions. That is more likely within
a marriage rather than a partnership; a good deal depends on how
much the woman's depth of old-fashioned feeling has survived even
the decision to take up partnership.

The changes in general conditions, especially as to housing, patterns of work and of leisure (with television as the most consuming
element here)—all these will encourage the nuclear rather than the
extended family, and will alter some of the terms of neighbourliness.
In more prosperous areas, among the former 'working class',
neighbourliness will be not so much a response to common need
but will survive, growing somewhat nearer the lower-middle-class
model, learning some of its language and habits. Neighbourly idioms and habits will be as relevant as ever in the 'sink' areas; but will
find it even harder to survive. Almost universal poverty will discourage that, and will on present showing remain.

4

Family and Neighbourhood (II)

If it wasn't for meat and good drink, the women might gnaw the sheets.
(Proverbial, but not in our area; too raucous)

Food

In the last half-century changes in attitudes towards the family and food are considerable, not as striking as those towards marriage, but very important. Earlier, one sign of a competent wife and mother was that she was proud to 'keep a good table', which didn't of course remotely mean that she went in for *haute cuisine* or anything like that. It meant rather that within the limits of her purse she regularly managed to put nourishing dishes on the table; plain probably, but 'tasty' (a key word) and 'filling' (the second key word). That also usually had to mean that the husband was in good regular work, or some 'skimping' would have to be done. The need is felt all the time to 'keep body and soul together' in the wage-earner. The two key words explain the fondness for strong sauces, as when a workman in a café lathers H.P. or Brown Sauce on to his bacon and other meats. In another sense, lack of 'taste' leads to the mass consumption of industrialised sausages and industrialised ice-cream, of hamburgers and frankfurters.

The contrast with today can be illustrated at an extreme by a recent event in a Midlands hospital. A youth in his late teens was in bed there after a motorcycle accident. The food, it was said by another patient, was not bad as hospitals go; that patient managed to eat it. The young man would have none of it. Instead his mother brought in each day McDonald's hamburgers. She said that was all he would eat at home. Whether she had tempted him with other things seems unlikely. She had accepted his choice and indeed seemed to find nothing questionable in the diet. The nurses in turn

59

seemed to think it not part of their job to coax him to widen his taste. His behaviour was starker, but not untypical of the general run of change.

My grandmother, from that large family in Boston Spa, found work at the local Squire's at about thirteen. Once married she came, after a spell in Arbroath, to Leeds with a growing family; her husband was in heavy engineering and Leeds was a magnet for that work. This would have been about three-quarters of the way through the nineteenth century or a little later. They settled in a great area of mainly terraced back-to-back houses, built to the South of the city to house the workers in the heavy industries, most of those just down on 'the main road' (the common phrase for the nearest artery which housed shops and often the trams; this one led towards Wakefield and London). Eventually there were ten children, and money was always tight.

I joined them in early 1927, when Grandma was in her seventies; and was 'struck' by the food. Our mother, who had just died, had had to feed four on £1 a week, so her provisioning had to be exceptionally controlled. By contrast, Grandma, with five or eventually six to cater for could, though not at all 'flush', provide the cheaper cuts of meat fairly regularly; and fish, chiefly cod; not fowl, for chicken was a luxury dish then, but rabbit and tripe, and a bit of bacon for Sunday breakfast. Sunday tea, especially if we had visitors (who were almost always 'family'), was the highlight, usually with tinned salmon and tinned 'fruit salad'. That was a range I had not known before.

It was a range which operated within a well-known set of rules. We rarely had a joint of meat, whether beef or lamb or pork; and those we had, perhaps on Sunday, were still the cheaper cuts; no sirloin or rump, of course. During the week, no pork or lamb chops, because they were comparatively expensive. We had tasty stews with dumplings, or fish, always 'white fish' and likely to be cod, which was hawked round on a handcart. Fresh salmon was out-of-reach; we could not have envisaged a time when that—farmed—was cheaper than some of our ordinary fish. Then there was offal, especially liver or kidneys For breakfast there was porridge or, more likely, bread with pork or beef dripping and their jelly, depending on what we had had for Sunday dinner. Corn-flakes were already available and, within a limited range, had been for some time; but not for us. That really did seem a wasteful way of eating. We didn't use the word 'processed', but that, as a suspicious idea, already lay at the back of our minds.

To a growing boy especially those meals always seemed good, without the help of Bisto, Oxo or any of their competitors. Like most Yorkshire housewives Grandma was a dab hand with Yorkshire puddings, also very tasty and a good filler-out to complement the meat side of things. She made her own pies, bread and cakes—especially sponge-cakes and teacakes—weekly; and her oven-bottom cakes were a boy's dream.

In short, she had a solidly built-in sense of good plain cooking, on the whole healthy, and within firm cash-limits quite well varied. Where did she almost subcutaneously pick up all this? Perhaps partly in the Big House, not from the food prepared for above-stairs but more likely from what the cook provided for downstairs. Since they were not a shiftless family, she would have learned even more from her mother about providing a range of good food on what she would not have called, but was, a shoestring.

The majority of housewives in those streets knew these things, too; they formed part of their invisible dowry. Many young women may then have come to marriage not greatly aware of its sex side (Grandma's oldest daughter had found 'all that' an unpleasant shock after marrying—but went on to have eleven children). They were much more likely to have been told that 'the way to a man's heart is through his stomach'.

Grandma would buy potted meat occasionally because making that could be too fussy for a busy housewife and Dawes down on the main road made very good stuff. A Dawes' granddaughter, perhaps the first to do so, came to University, to Birmingham to read English. She brought me a packet of their potted beef, Proust's madeleine. In general Grandma dismissed 'shop-boughten' confectionery. Most Hunslet confectioners could not afford to be in the first rank. One soon learned the difference, could recognise the types: garish, artificially coloured on top, and the taste. They appear in the windows of the cheaper chain-bakers-and-confectioners who, their electronic machines visible at the back of the shops, have sprung up in the last few decades; and whose recipes owe less to 'good home baking' than to accountants' calculations of what level of ingredients will best serve 'the bottom line' without losing trade.

Among the usual idioms about eating appeared some pseudo-polite rebukes, especially in the more self-respecting households:

'Well, I suppose fingers came before forks' (that comes from the 16th century, via Swift's *Polite Conversation*), as someone passed a slice of bread over by hand. More frequent were some already met in a related context: 'Your eyes are bigger than your belly'; or, more indulgently, of 'a growing lad': 'He eats like a horse these days', and perhaps, also indulgently: 'He's got a real sweet tooth'. The breadwinner was entitled to 'the lion's share', but perhaps was given to 'making a pig of himself'. Some, at a time when they were rather straitened, might intone, from Cicero, 'hunger is the best sauce'; followed by 'enough is as good as a feast', 'half a loaf is better than no bread' (16th century), 'you'll eat me out of house and home', and inevitably 'waste not, want not.' For a few housewives the standard rebuke from her neighbours was : 'She's a lazy ha'porth. Her husband never sees a square meal from one week's end to the other'.

There comes to mind at this point another range of rather odd sayings about food which do seem to be characteristically working class: 'They're always feeding their faces' (of a greedy family); 'there's nowt spoiling' (to a latecomer for a meal); 'it'll put you on' (a snack till the meal is ready); and 'siding' (clearing the table after a meal or to prepare for one).

All this recalls smells, especially those of food mixed with all the more humdrum household smells, and often marked by the days of the week. On Mondays, the smell of damp but gently steaming washing round the fire because it was raining, on a warmth-stealing clothes-horse, mixed with the smell of yesterday's meat served cold or re-heated, with bubble-and-squeak (not one of my favourites). On Thursdays or Fridays, again according to the weather, the 'bottoming' of the downstairs room with the smell of carbolic soap in the suds of the wet scrubbing-brush, mixed with the tastebud-tempting smell of baking, especially of those oven-cakes.

The outside smells were chiefly, during the week, from a few different kinds of cooking and, at ground level, the sooty smell of grass in mucky earth forcing its way through the cobblestones. At week-ends, the smell of virtually identical Sunday dinners permeated the whole street until mid-afternoon; by late evening, Woodbines and pee (especially near the dog-spattered lamp-posts) predominated. De Rezke were regarded as a slightly smarter cigarette; Woodbines were the English working-man's Gaulois. One thing we never smelled in those days was 'grass', 'coke'. But enough of that kind of recollecting; it soon becomes an indulgence.

And today? It is easy to use the past to belabour the present, especially when great changes are taking place. Most changes underway now are due to that widely diffused greater prosperity, and this has clearly brought benefits. Those are often noted; especially by those whose profits depend on the rest of us being persuaded to think all is for the best in the best of all possible worlds, their Panglossian subjects; the costs are not so much assessed.

Since so large a proportion of women go out to work nowadays they cannot have anything like as much time for cooking as their mothers had. To cater for them, though not only for that group, the supermarkets in particular provide an ever-increasing range of prepared foods in brilliantly enticing packing. Some of them almost live up to the promise of the packets. The promotions for most of them are increasingly following the ingratiating 'Go on. Indulge Yourself' line (at Sainsbury's, 'Be Good to Yourself', which is slightly more modestly English, more suitable for approaching those prosperous customers who remain cautious of 'indulgence'). Sainsbury's have also introduced a new range of meals somewhat dearer than their predecessors (which usually remain). The motto on the new packets is 'Taste the difference' and certainly most have more flavour than those now in the second division. It could backfire psychologically, by implicitly suggesting that what we have been offered so far wasn't as good as they could have made it, that they only pulled their fingers out when some bright spark in the Public Relations department dreamed up what seemed an irresistibly catching and so profitable 'come on' slogan.

Most prepared foods, regular or enhanced, are dearer than the same dishes prepared at home. But many housewives now not at home may be able to earn at work more than will pay for the extra cost of the prepared dishes. The balance can be spent on all sorts of things otherwise unavailable: a not-new car, a foreign holiday, a new or refurbished kitchen with not only a microwave but also a dishwasher. The TV would be there anyway; it is essential in even the poorer homes, whether the wife works or not and whether or not there is a husband. All this is understandable and in large measure justifiable.

We can all, if we will, now know that as a result of factory farming and increased competition most of our foods have progressively become cheaper. For that, we may pay an unexpected and unexpectedly high price. This is not yet fully or widely understood, but is moving nearer to the top of the agenda of social costs.

There are other, even less evident but almost as regrettable costs. Surveys have shown that many working wives today hardly know how to cook, let alone prepare, one of those 'square' meals. A pity on the whole; it can come in handy at least now and again; and to make even the simplest and of course tastiest things, such as a really stomach-lining soup or substantial fish-cakes—especially if you start those with tinned red sockeye salmon, or tuna—can be very enjoyable in itself.

It might be just as well to avoid also some of those chemicals whose names most of us cannot interpret but which occupy two or three lines in the obligatory lists of contents—the colour-enhancers and flavour-enhancers and preservatives and artificial sweeteners and this-or-that other chemical substitute. Look at the long list on the back of a plastic container of one of the most popular 'fruit drinks' with an engaging, ad-invented, suitably fruity, name. One favourite contains, hidden in a long list of other ingredients, 5 percent real fruit juice; children love it, of course, and most rushed-off-their-feet mothers are not inclined to argue about these things.

Nor about demands for Coca-Cola, that tarted-up version of sarsaparilla, which is less refreshing than dandelion-and-burdock. Has anyone done a thorough study of how Coke gained its hold? Having tasted it once or twice, and read its history, I find it is difficult to understand how that came about other than through promotion, though perhaps there is a 'secret ingredient' which is habit-forming. U.S. servicemen seem to be assumed unwilling to start fighting until they know that millions of bottles of Coke lie in reserve behind the line. Is it a supreme example of the power of marketing? That would be a sad conclusion, but may be correct.

Coca-Cola and McDonalds—the leaders in fast foods, followed by chicken, pizza and pasta chains—have by now corralled the taste of billions right across the globe. By comparison, fish-and-chips in beef dripping begins to seem like an example of high traditional taste.

This shift was illustrated at a social peak one evening on television, in a series on the life of a duke and duchess in their Great House. The duke was newly home after a gruelling heart operation. His wife reminded him that from now and for a long time his diet would be restricted to boiled fish and the like; in particular, nothing fried or greasy. The duke winced and asked for one final meal of the sort he loved, before the new regime began.

The duchess relented and left him lying on the suitably elegant settee in what might have been called the drawing- or sitting-room, and dashed in the Range Rover to the nearby motorway service area, for a burger with trimmings and a milk-shake. The duke ate with what looked something like rapture: 'Lovely!' The duchess asked how if at all it compared with the pleasure of a fine French meal. He thought the pleasure was about the same. One can just understand the duke's enjoyment of the burger; very occasionally, if travelling on my own, I indulge in one; they're 'real tasty'—but that pink milk-shake!

That cameo deserves to become a McDonald's commercial on TV; it encapsulates the classless appeal of the most popular fast food and drinks; and the fee might pay for a new roof to the stables.

Yet most broadsheets and fashionable magazines are united in saying often how much British eating-out has improved in the last two decades. Comparisons favourable to us are made with Paris. If you are able to pay what is now regarded as a reasonable minimum, say between £60 and £70 for two, you can, we are told, eat very well in London, Birmingham, Manchester, Leeds, Edinburgh, and some rural parts. That simply indicates the new social divisions; those establishments cater to the new meritocracy with their platinum credit cards.

For the middle range, there are simulacra, sad simulacra. In between the fast food outlets and the places just mentioned above, there are now national chains of what look like full-scale restaurants, with would-be French or imitation olde-English names and limp 'salad bars', aimed at people, most of whom do not know good cooking of any kind and are disinclined by native habit to object to frozen, industrialised stuff served by waitresses and waiters who, too, know nothing about good food or good wine; all in suitably plasticated fake interiors. Any Portuguese village can produce at least one restaurant whose honest, homely food far out-classes these places. This is the abyss of food and feeling, offered successfully by people whose obsessive interest is, like that of the industrialised confectioners, 'watching the bottom line' of whatever 'industry' they have put their money in, not the quality of their food; and whose contempt—unconscious?—for their customers is scarcely concealed but not often brought into question. The possibility of moving towards good cooking outside the home for all but the most prosperous has been hijacked. This recalls the late Cecil King, when asked to defend some of the rubbish he printed in his newspapers, answering with frank cynicism that only someone who published a popular newspaper knew how ignorant and gullible most English people are.

At least some Chinese and some Indian restaurants, especially if owned and run by a family, know what they are about—as to the food itself. There are some pubs, probably an increasing number, that have rediscovered respectable English cooking, sometimes at reasonable prices. Best to buy a guide to them, though. The last time we went into one which advertised on the road outside its 'fine home cooking' we were given frozen stuff no doubt shuttled in by a white van from a mass caterer on a nearby industrial estate, and shoved in the microwave: the chips tasted of greasy cardboard and the breaded plaice had turned up its tail in despair. Obviously their advert was a lie, but that would not have occurred to them; jargon sales-phrases are assumed to have their own kind of 'truth' and justification. We left most of our portions, and the waitress did not question that; everyone else there chewed away stolidly.

As so often, those in the underclass come off worst in all this. The mother in a one-parent home is less likely than others to be in even part-time work; she hasn't much money to spend. She could save considerably by making her own meals and buying fresh fruit, trying as hard as possible not to yield to the pressure from the children to buy hamburgers or those invented 'fruit drinks'. But the culture of the streets and the school playgrounds is against her, and the advertisers know and encourage this. Perhaps the broadcasters, even if the advertisers didn't like it, would put on programmes which didn't seem to aim at the hospitality-aspirations of those slightly better-off, and would mount a series for those socially and financially lower down. Relatively few might watch them, but they would be a 'fit audience though few'. That would certainly be Public Service Broadcasting.

The imitation restaurants are among the newer temptations, and aimed slightly above more traditionally minded working-class people, which reminds us that 'class' is above all a state of mind. Some older habits, and those not always healthy, seem not to have lost their hold among a great many in the working class. In many homes the 'fry-up', preferably with chips, still dominates. Outside, it may be often called 'brunch' today but that's a bit of P.R. from across the Atlantic. Again, the cafés in the supermarkets, together with the motorway chains and some in the towns and cities, lead the way. A large extension was not long ago built to our biggest supermarket so the usual clientele of the café was swollen by the builders during their breaks.

The 'fry-up' might have been inscribed for decades or perhaps centuries at the top of some ur-English menu and strongly survives, passed on from father to son along with fidelity to the local football team and the saloon-bar pint: bacon and eggs ('two eggs or one?'), beans or tomatoes—tinned—('both, please'), two sausages (usually more cereal and seasoning than meat), fried bread and perhaps, again from the States, hash-brown triangles instead of or in addition to chips, and, latest of all, a brilliant would-be traditional touch from the marketing department, a slice of black pudding. Yes, it's all extremely tasty; but many workmen on our building-site had it on most days. The arteries must feel continuously coagulated, thick and burpy.

Recently we met a young woman living in partnership with a hire-car driver. She was deeply attached and doing what to her seemed best for him: 'I see him off every day with a good cooked breakfast—two eggs, bacon, fried bread and sausage'. That's slightly attenuated in comparison with Sainsbury's and Tesco's brunch, but dangerously loving.

A recent 'Holiday' series on television focused on a Lancashire working-class family's first visit abroad, to Benidorm. Over the first lunch in their self-catering apartment, the mother had provided an enormous fry-up; the local supermarket obviously stocked all the favourite English ingredients. The mother was enormous too and the children going that way. It was made poignant as much as sad since those parents' parents were probably not at all well-off so that a big fry-up would have been only for special occasions. Yet here was the next generation holidaying abroad and able if they wished to have a fry-up every day. A sort of Eldorado.

Our supermarket café was recently demolished in favour of a shiny transatlantic coffee bar, which sells not brunch but varieties of expensive coffees with croissants and the like. The experts on profit-margins have won the day, but perhaps will inadvertently encourage healthier eating, unless we desert them for the other supermarket down the road. After a month the new place is trading poorly; high prices and no bacon sandwiches are winning, which is a slight compensation.

Each weekday morning the young mothers from the council-estate across the road take their children to the nearby school. Few of them seem to be of the underclass, nor to be sole parents; there is much confident chatter within and between groups. About a quarter seem overweight, and half of those greatly overweight. One can easily see from the traces on their faces alone that only a few years ago most were likely to have been slim and physically attractive. What has happened? Has their diet been badly skewed, especially since marriage? Have they not been very active about the house? There were a few fat housewives in Hunslet, but the dominant look was lean, from rushing about in an overall or pinny on daily chores; there could be little snack-eating and no sitting in snatches during the day watching television.

This is the sort of observation which angers some people. They would be less angry if the unhealthy state were put down wholly to political misjudgment or lack of good advice at school or the wickedness of the supermarkets and their advertisers rather than, at least in part, to choices made by individuals. Such an easy judgment reduces people. The condition is not new. Hunslet had a language for it, quite unevasive: 'since she got wed and especially since she had the kids *she's let 'erself go'*.

Drink

For a very long time drink was, apart from the danger of 'the sack', the greatest fear of the respectable working-classes. It hung over many threatened households as heavily as the mortgage repayments can elsewhere. It was also for many, especially men, the greatest relief, escape. No other element contained more contradictions.

Drink could be 'the road to ruin'. Even there, gin was popularly known as 'mother's ruin', but we did not hear that often. There were a few women round about known to be addicted to gin, but only one or two. The expression conjured up for me in adolescence Hogarth's *Gin Lane* and the drunken woman dropping her child. In general, women did not drink as much as men, and from other women those who drank regularly and heavily drew pity more than scorn. Men who took to drink were in danger of bringing the house down, from reasonable living to penury. 'He's taken to drink' rang like a doom-laden bell. Some did that out of weakness, lack of 'backbone', and some because they were 'driven to it', perhaps by a nagging wife or the constant and increasing fear of 'the sack' or a bullying boss or back-breaking work or the pressure of their mates. Whatever the cause, their addiction could soon threaten to lead to 'rack and ruin'. A man who 'couldn't keep his beer down', who soon had had 'one too many' and showed it disgustingly, was scorned more than pitied.

A few phrases indicated a toleration of drink and even some amusement, which is why so many drunks, often wrapped around lampposts, figured in the postcard cartoons of Donald McGill. 'Drunk as a lord' they might say and the origins of that are not hard to find though unlikely to be used today. Then came: ' 'e's been wetting his whistle (16th- century 'throat') alright'; and the reverse: ' 'e's as sober as a judge'—another aware of well-recognised older hierarchies.

Stalybridge liked to tell the tale of a drunken man walking up the middle of a street and realising that some of the housewives were watching him from their lintels. He stopped and harangued them to this effect: 'Shame on you, women; have you no washing, no baking, no cooking, that you should waste time watching a drunken man going up your way!'

I can recall only about a dozen of the regular phrases that accompanied working-class drinking: 'Tight as a tick', 'pissed', 'half-pissed', 'pissed up to his eyeballs', 'pissed as a newt', 'one over the eight; 'one too many', 'half-seas over'; and prefaced by 'what are 'ye having?' and—especially much later—by 'cheers', which as we saw earlier has escaped from its class of origin, the middle, and become ubiquitous and multipurpose.

There is a painful story about L. H. Myers and Orwell and their difficulty in making contact. Myers was willing to give Orwell some help with money. They went into a pub and Orwell asked Myers what he would like. Myers answered in a way which indicated that he did not know the correct language of the saloon-bar culture and Orwell corrected him brusquely. A pity, that: Orwell had chosen to learn it as part of his effort to shuck-off his Etonian background; Myers didn't have to.

One does not often hear in working-class bars phrases such as: 'Bottoms up', 'have one on me', 'my turn, I think,' 'the sun's over the yard-arm' (that naval remnant usually means six p.m., was honoured by Auden and still is by many another), 'what about the other half?', or 'the hair of the dog?' (drawn from the supposition that the burnt hair of a dog could counter drunkenness), and—frowned on today—'one for the road'. Most drinking idioms still stick to their own class.

In earlier days one met on entering many a pub the mixed smell of beer and fags; today one is more likely, especially in the big cities and the not-predominantly working-class bars, to meet that of wine and drugs.

Health

It is 'common knowledge', though not widely enough admitted, that on the whole the health of working-class people before both of this century's major wars was much poorer than that of those in better-off groups. It had become a national scandal on each occasion when doctors, examining men for military service, realised how bad the health of most of them was. In the forties the greater size of most U.S. servicemen came as a shock. The sense of scandal has since faded, with not much justification The root cause was and is bad diet, lack of exercise and of fresh air, all earlier compounded by lack of sufficient money. We come back to the paradox: greater prosperity has not led in general to healthier eating, but rather to greater consumption of less healthy foods. As one result, the National Health Service is always chasing its own tail, not able to give much attention to preventive medicine.

One result of this discovery during the Second World War was the issuing to children of milk and orange juice. Again, we do not always give credit to those decisions carried through for the better health of children even during a war. A very cheering decision, inspired partly by hard logic, partly by compassion. It was all too obvious that not enough fruit was eaten, not enough milk drunk. Families with 'something about them' (meaning 'wits') and enough money would provide cocoa, porridge, prunes; but very many didn't and weren't greatly encouraged to do so. It was a disgrace to one of the wealthiest societies in the world, and a sign of its near-fatal social divisiveness. That 'eating a peck of dirt before you die' adage applied especially to places like Hunslet, given their polluted air.

Mrs. Thatcher's much later decision, as Secretary of State for Education, to stop the issue of free milk in schools, was shameful. It is hard to imagine how a minister with those duties, and presumably with knowledge of the historic record on the health of the poor, let alone the opportunity to assess conditions in Grantham from the family's grocery shop, could have come to that decision; and have it supported by the Cabinet. Perhaps it was founded in the belief that working-class children could have had milk and oranges if their parents hadn't squandered money, probably on drink; if so, all the children were then paying for a false assumption about most of their parents. Even if the assumption had been well-founded it would have been inhumane.

The thirties were the period of rambling and hiking and biking but those health-giving recreations, with few exceptions, started somewhere in the lower-middle-classes, or in the aspirant respectable working-class.

To the poor health of many, smoking and drinking added their part and so did the lack of dental care. Teeth tended to rot early. Many a man or woman had lost all their teeth before they were thirty; some, losing them one by one, decided early to 'have done with it'; and 'be rid of them all''. Nowadays you may not recognise that even a neighbour you have known for years has a full denture. Not in the thirties; the broad smile of cheap, 'Panel', gnashers had the excessive glow of a pale sun rising on a poster for Bridlington Bay.

It need not be, and in some ways is not like that today; but the reorganisation (not at all the 'reform') of the National Dental Service a few years ago is bringing back some of the earlier widespread neglect, especially among poorer people. Delays for treatment under the national service are increasing as dentists opt for the more lucrative private practice. Free treatment is not now available to many who could claim it before; they are now assumed to be able to afford it. In a perfectly logical world, perhaps they could. But many no longer include dental care in their budgeting; there are always a great many other things on which you are obliged to spend your often limited money; and some things you are not obliged to spend it on but do. Of course, if you belong to the Thatcherite persuasion, you will sternly say: 'That's their look-out'; charity had and has a narrow brief there.

The decline of good sight is not always evident in most people's early years. But a milkiness in the eyes not long after sixty used to be very common. There, there has been an evident gain. Cataracts can be removed, and Glaucoma if tackled early can be sometimes controlled. The crowded eye clinics in many hospitals, and very often the long waiting-lists, indicate how much is now being done and, perhaps, that more people are concerned when their sight begins to deteriorate than about the state of their teeth.

That is understandable; we would miss our eyes more than our teeth. And hearing? Concern about that seems to come somewhere between the other two; not as bothersome as loss of sight, but more than loss of teeth. One sees a fair-sized group of over-sixties fiddling with the prominent, whistling, non-digital, National Health hearing aids; many seem just to put up with the loss, until both ears are affected. Better-off people buy unobtrusive, digital, vastly expensive electronic aids which are elaborate tiny computers; a very prosperous business indeed, greatly nourished by advertising which is anything but unobtrusive.

Many adages about health are euphemisms, devices for not admitting much: 'I'm in the pink, thanks', 'fit as a fiddle' and, less commonly, 'right as a trivet' (a three-legged stool). Conversely, 'a bit off colour' covers most publicly-declared needs; more detailed and graphic accounts tend to be reserved for family, friends and close neighbours. One such common and foreboding phrase, especially among middle-aged and older women, was:"I've just had a nasty/funny turn" (a dizzy spell). On the whole, one was not much aware of hypochondriacs; or didn't know the word.

Local markets used to cater for some of the antique beliefs in, especially, herbal cures. Some you took home, some were drunk on the spot. Some survive, though many have become sophisticated as wings of Alternative Medicine, with prices which have risen appropriately. Alleged cures for gallstones were prominent and the recovered stones sometimes put in a bottle on the living-room mantelpiece, as souvenirs of the great pains now happily dissolved-away.Which were due to the fairground quacks and which to the ministrations of 'proper' doctors was not clear.

From what has been said earlier about the food chosen by many people today it is plain that the differences in health between classes largely remain. Perhaps they are not as large as they used to be; rickets and some of the rest—beginning with 'nits'—have gone or been much reduced. Vaccination has helped and better advice in schools; better advice generally. Other forces, as we have seen, work in different directions. The improvement, especially for the worse off, is not at all as considerable as it should have been. 'Two steps forward, one and a half back.'

Weather, the Countryside, and the Time of Year

This small section was prompted by realising how many, among the great many adages about health, recall centuries ago, when we were forced to be even more conscious than we are today about the weather. Natural disasters such as floods apart, we grumble about the weather more as an inconvenience, a disruption, a nuisance, which

can interrupt holidays and weekend trips, but not damage the liveli-
hoods of most of us It may, of course, in winter bring on influenza
and bronchial ailments which 'take off' many. In that sense we still
almost automatically relate weather to health.

In my childhood we regularly invoked epigrams which sprang
from a different sort of life than ours. We spoke of 'February fill-
dyke', when we hadn't seen a dyke for years; we intoned that 'March
comes in like a lion and goes out like a lamb', and that 'April show-
ers bring May flowers' when we were lucky if we had a window-box
with a few nasturtiums in it or just possibly a few municipal-looking
geraniums; we insisted that we shouldn't 'cast a clout till May is out'.
Sometimes we fully followed the old ways. If bronchitis threatened in
late Winter my grandmother spread goose-grease on a sheet of brown
paper and pressed that to my chest, where it stayed for a few weeks.

We met earlier that linkage of ducks and bad weather which so
puzzled our Austrian landlady. That was due chiefly to the strange
obliquity and ironic inflections dear to English speech; no doubt the
Austrians too have many epigrams about the weather; though more
direct, perhaps; less duck-related

We cling especially to rhyme: 'Red sky at night, shepherds de-
light'—hollow, empty, merely a tired, out-of-date and lazy repetition? Probably. But when my Grandma said it, it seemed to echo
something from childhood; a distant connection was still being made,
though probably unconsciously. Add 'the North wind doth blow /
And we shall have snow' and 'rain before seven, fine before eleven'
(a peculiarly strange bit of optimistic folklore. I expect the forecast-
ers today could tell us if there is any scientific basis for it). The neat
confidence of 'When the wind is in the East / Good for neither man
nor beast' is pleasant and probably well-founded.

As has become clear more than once, it seems odd that such sayings regularly ranged through those streets; odd to us nowadays,
but not then, to them. It has become inescapably clear that memories of another kind of life lingered and linger in our language much
more than we have been used to realising. Meanwhile also, the
younger children sang in the playground 'Rain, rain, go away / Come
again another day'. The innocent-sounding music of that lingers
also; but perhaps only just survives. as snatches from television tunes
and rhymes take over.

One of the oddest and still mildly current epigrams in this group
is puzzling since it can be taken in at least two ways; perhaps that is

why it lingers—a double-purpose tool: 'Feed a cold and starve a fever'. It can be taken as a serious warning: 'If you feed someone with a cold, you will end by inducing a fever in them'; or as a piece of sound positive advice: 'You should feed someone with a cold, but starve them if they have a fever'. The second seems more likely. It seems likely also that different people use it differently.

*   *   *

To recapitulate:

Meanwhile, most drinking idioms survive and, except for an odd stray, stick to their class. Food and eating have undergone changes almost as great as changes in the attitude to marriage; it is plain that the two have links. Many old aphorisms here have lost relevance, their hold on reality. You would not often hear today about the value of 'good home-cooking', of the importance of 'keeping a good table', or of seeing that 'your man' left home in the morning with a good meal 'under his belt'; the wife too is likely to be getting ready to leave for work New phrases are not aphorisms but brisk single utterances: 'Nip down and get us a pizza'; though that had its antecedent in times when things were rushed and corners being cut, and can still be heard 'Run down to the chippie and get fish and chips three times' has carried over.

Since on the whole the more public aspects of health-care—eyes, ears, teeth—have seen improvements, we are likely to hear less of them in aphorisms. A few market-quacks remain, their nostrums still 'sworn by' by some; their kind of hold can be almost as strong as that of soothsayers, fortune-tellers.

Aphorisms about more recent health preoccupations—cervical or breast or prostate cancer, for example—are yet to be created. Probably enough of the old ones will serve well enough to be applied to those for a long time to come. Most of the older less specific ones will also long continue to serve; such as: 'You can tell by her face that she hasn't long to go.'

We talk in aphorisms about the weather much as we ever did, and are likely to go on doing so.

5

Family and Neighbourhood (III)

*A good fence helpeth to keep peace between neighbours; but let us take heed
that we make not a high stone wall, to keep us from meeting.*
                                                        —*Proverbial; c.1640*

Neighbours

It is easy, and misleading, to give the impression that the sense of
neighbourliness exists almost entirely within the working class. Live
in a middle-class district for a while and you will realise that that
sense is traditionally very strong there also. Helping you to settle in
when you first arrive; offering help if there is illness in the house,
with shopping if your car breaks down, in swapping gardening tools
and exchanging plants; all this and much else is ingrained within the
culture. There's not much dropping in for a gossip or half a pound
of sugar, though. On the other hand an extended form of
neighbourliness, unpaid voluntary good works within the community, is much more a middle-class than a working-class tradition. For
obvious reasons.

The strong sense of neighbourliness in pre-war working-class life
was not so much a willing voluntary option as it might be elsewhere,
something your kind were used to doing freely and were glad to do.
In working-class life it was also part of the structure of things, a
necessity rather than an option, a buttress, within the seam of day-
by-day living, something you almost had to rely on or life would
have become much more difficult.

There were exceptions, of course, people who did not mix, who
kept their doors shut and lived within themselves, within their own
families, nuclear or extended. They were 'the sort who wouldn't
give you the time of day'. A nice use of the word 'give'. Sometimes
that arose from shyness, sometimes from suspicion by or of her; in

75

which last instance a guiding motto might be, about someone near by: 'You can tell her by the company she keeps', or, even more forbidding, as a pair of neighbours were seen gossiping: 'It takes one to know one'. Or she may be simply mean, the sort of person who was forever muttering 'That'll always come in' as she pocketed some trifle. But for most, neighbourliness was the main lubricant which oiled many of the local wheels.

There was no, or not much, sense of personal space outside the front door, so for good and sometimes ill the emergence of neighbourliness was rooted in another, a restraining, lack, had its reverse side; and emphasized the importance of being able to 'shut your own front door', to close off the packed street-world outside, neighbourly or not.

Conversely again, it was part of the received, the orthodox, wisdom that you had to help each other, that this was almost essential to survival. There we were, there we had to be. We took for granted, without uttering them, complex and quite subtle rules of engagement, especially as to those lines it was best not to cross; and those which demanded unquestioned instant attention. Of these last, one of the most emblematic was that of knocking with a poker on your fireback (if you shared your chimney-breast with a neighbour, as in terrace-houses) to indicate that the baby had started coming and the local midwife had better be called quickly, or the husband or wife had had a stroke or heart attack; or some other emergency.

The single most important fact of life that encouraged the neighbourly spirit in working-class people was that you could hardly ever afford to pay for services from elsewhere. To put up with things which were not quite right, to 'make do' and 'make shift', not to expect too much, to ensure that a little went along way: all these were deeply engrained in the spirit, a bottom layer of unspoken assumptions.

So you 'helped each other out'. You, as if automatically, exchanged jobs that one or the other of you could carry out properly. Sometimes cash was involved, but more usual was a form of bargaining or barter, the exchange of services rather than of money, or of goods, though those could be involved. Most would have in their heads a list of people in nearby streets, often but by no means always men, who would do a bit of plumbing or carpentry or electrical repairs, repairs you knew the landlord would 'take an age' in doing. If pay was involved, it would usually be little. This practice therefore helped, if only in a small way, to encourage petty pilfering from works and shops, to get the stuff to do the job, in particular. For many years after moving to a more prosperous world, some could find it slightly unnerving, an extravagant gesture, to 'phone for a carpenter or decorator'.

You simply had to 'stick together'; 'a friend in need is a friend indeed' (that has what seems like a distinctively English sound, a line of folk poetry; in much the same form it comes up from Cicero and Seneca and others). What a treat it is to note these interleavings of languages and centuries feeding our tongues, unconsciously: 'one good turn deserves another'—that might seem relatively late here; the French had it from at least the early 14th century.

Men had their close communities, the mates at work or 'down the Pub/Club'. Women were the living heart of the neighbourly spirit; that was their kind of club. Naturally, the degrees of coming together varied greatly, chiefly according to character. Some were 'thick as thieves' with a chosen few; with them they 'would go through hell and high water', 'share their last crust'; they 'got on like a house on fire', were 'hand in glove', always saw 'eye to eye'. Each would be likely to swear that the other—one of the greatest compliments—'hadn't a mean bone in her body'. No one would be likely actually to admit that their bosom friend was, as perhaps the speaker might herself be, rather ungenerous, someone who 'blows hot and cold', 'leaves a bad taste in the mouth'. She was likely to be, rather, 'the salt of the earth'.

At the far, other end of the line were those briefly mentioned earlier, who hardly mixed or made close contacts at all. They were not necessarily unpleasant people, more likely to be family-centred, perhaps rather withdrawn, the wife by nature bent on 'keeping herself to herself', or even discouraged by her husband from much mixing around the neighbourhood. They had thresholds few slipped over, no matter how short they happened to be on sugar or tea. The congenital borrowers knew exactly who belonged to that group or, rather, line of individuals; so did the individuals.

Somewhere in between were the modest-mixers, such as my mother-in-law. Good neighbours, especially when urgent help was needed, on good enough terms with almost everybody, someone who would 'always give you the time of day' politely enough, but would rarely linger for a 'natter' or 'a good cal'—perhaps that word, the idiomatic synonym for gossip, might best have two 'l's; we noted before that its 'a' is certainly flat.

Also, in between the inveterates and the 'not over my threshold's' were a few other types, all well recognised. Someone who has revealed herself as no more than 'a fair weather friend' would soon be disclosed and soon, if not cold-shouldered, at least not encouraged. Nor would the 'really common' woman, the slut whose 'name is mud' because she had now been revealed 'for what she is', one whose ways 'stick in most other people's gullets'. 'No love was lost' on them. Underneath, neighbourliness could have severe regulations; not all who live near become neighbours in the full sense; admission to membership was not all that easy.

So there were accepted and implied distinctions between the three main kinds of relationships, though they could overlap. There was the family, often the extended family, and often gathered within only a few neighbouring streets; that had pride of place unless there had been serious rifts. Later, council rehousing could put strains on usual custom. In the middle were the neighbours who, obviously, lived very near; though particularly good neighbourly friendships could just survive some movings away, but not too far.

Unsurprisingly, staying in each other's houses was rare, unless in an emergency. You had to be quite 'close' for that. Less close arrangements could be made if both sides 'got on well'. After Grandma died, I lived with one of my aunts for a while; the only ones left of the old household. It was simply assumed that that would be, from then until I finally detached myself, 'home'. We soon moved to Armley where Aunt Clara and her friend set about running the women's outfitters they had set up. They did not have much time to spare for feeding a young man during the day. Arrangements were made for the days I was not up at the University, for me to have the midday meal, 'dinner', with the elderly woman opposite. She was 'a treasure', kind and cheerful. Her husband was a retired Council worker and their children were scattered. She asked 1/- (5p); for a piled dish of 'meat-and-two vegetables', or meat-and-potato pie, or cottage- or shepherd's-pie, or liver and mash or fish, and a filling pudding. She was a model of the best sort of wife and mother and neighbour of that kind of area.

Holidays away from home were rare, except for those in regular work. The father of a boy opposite us was a foreman and 'doing alright'; they went to Blackpool for a week every year, which put them 'a peg or two' above the rest, and we were envious. Self-help could come in here, though. Some members of the extended family might live in another big town a few score miles away, or even in the country. Then, so long as you were 'on good terms', you could have holidays not officially organised as exchanges, but still a form of mutual transfer. Some of ours, though not many, would come from Sheffield to Leeds and vice-versa. We seemed to have no country cousins.

But we habitually found remarkable and intriguing differences between Sheffield and Leeds, respectively, differences which would be imperceptible to, say, a Londoner. The town centres in particular were as distinctive to us as are the town centres of foreign lands to more 'travelled' people; as distinct from each other as Milan and Turin, or Frankfurt and Munich or Strasbourg and Lyons.

The third group of relationships was with 'friends' and here we can note striking differences between classes. Those of the professional classes can certainly have good neighbourly relations in some of the ways suggested above—to help things along in a friendly way, but not as part of a complicated, regular, assumed, *need* to give actual physical help to each other. They also, the professional middle classes, have friends to an extent rare and rather different from those among the working classes. Friends do not necessarily live close by; in fact, most of them in the nature of things probably do not. They are not in any practical definition neighbours who live very near, and do not inevitably become 'psychological neighbours'. They are friends, perhaps made at work by the husband or wife, or introduced to each other through the friends made by their children at school, or by contacts at church or in those voluntary bodies that so proliferate in middle-class districts, or by mutual recreational interests from golf to bridge. They are likely to have their own car or cars and to give dinner parties (or 'have people to supper') to those within their own circle as well as to professional contacts. Friendships such as these, especially when the children are still at school, can extend to common holidays. Nowadays there is for children a complicated network of 'sleep-overs', and birthday parties of increasing elaboration at recommended places in town (such as bowling alleys). Friendship is therefore complicated and of course has its rules, but, and these are the crucial differences, it does not, except to a relatively small degree, regularly rely on mutual support (though, as we have already seen, that will be forthcoming if necessary) and it is more expensive to maintain than 'neighbourliness' could normally be; intrinsic to the old style of neighbourliness had to be the knowledge that it cost nothing or almost nothing.

One might say that, after family, neighbours, and friends, there were 'acquaintances', but one heard that word only rarely in working-class districts. It seemed to belong to another social world and few among us used it. That aunt who had served in a moderately 'better class' shop occasionally brought this world into the house. It always seemed like a stranger come among us from a more genteel world, a linguistic whiff of that favourite scent Lily of the Valley, or perhaps Eau de Cologne; but not Phulnana; that would have been 'common', 'real Woolworths', even to us. So the progression 'acquaintance to friend' was on the whole alien.

In all these relationships, it is obvious, there were fine, largely unarticulated but firmly understood distinctions. Those within the spider's webs of neighbourliness were no less complex than the others.

Gossip

To be more charitable than most gossips deserve: it can start in the practice of anecdotage, which many of us love; it acquires spice and so invokes a complicity between gossiper and hearer. Gossip could run like a virus—human foot and mouth disease, say, transferred through the interplay of both—running with various degrees of disabling strength through a working-class neighbourhood; propinquity made it travel quickly. It always 'comes out', it spreads like a stain, or it may submerge for a time, then, like a message in a bottle washed up on the shore, it surfaces again.

It was not eradicable; that would have been against nature and most of it in most places was not highly poisonous; self-indulgent and time-wasting, rather, though sometimes malicious; and enjoying a relish for the whiff of scandal and the warm breath of *schadenfreude;* those could be corrosive. One virulent 'gossip' (the person not the event) could sour a whole district. Luckily, most people could spot them; but some suffered. Was so-and-so's daughter really pregnant (probably by her boyfriend but, more awkwardly, perhaps by her immediate boss) and getting ready to hide that in one way or another; was Mrs. so-and-so having an affair with the insurance-man; was Mr. so-and-so 'in the black books' at work because of goods gone missing? 'There's no smoke without fire', 'he's a dark one', and 'I always thought he/she was no better than he/she should be' (that sounds home-grown, almost contemporary; actually, it is first found in the early 17th century).

That cluster of adages which invoke the devil was much in evidence though it had become debilitated with use and some of its forms sounded no worse than calling a suspicious person 'a bad 'un'. Some of those pairs of women on the pavement, arms crossed over their pinnies, were well-practised in the conventional body-gestures of the conspiratorial 'a nod's as good as a wink' (probably late 15th century) and 'between you and me and the gate-post' (an alternative is 'bed-post', which we never used. Prudery?). They employed especially the eyes and the side of the mouth as they changed register to deliver, *sotto voce,* a particularly smelly and juicy piece of scandal—these pairs or trios had to be circumvented as you came back from school and perhaps gave them a quizzical; 'Good afternoon, ladies.' ('cheeky young sod!' or 'toffee-nosed young snob!'). Les Dawson captured that best, though one or two others were also masters of the 'Oo, missus! You don't say!' mode as, with arms bent at the elbows, they hitched-up their 'bust-bodices'. No wonder some housewives decided even more firmly to 'keep themselves to themselves'.

When clothes-lines ran across the street (they almost disappeared when council housing provided semis with a strip of back-garden); that too was a favourite venue for gossip. Today a main site is among the aisles of the supermarkets. Many women, not only those from the middle class, have mobile phones. It is puzzling that they seem to have to use them so often in there, though one can invent a few reasons. But they can easily co-exist with face-to-face gossip, in-the-aisles chat. A newer kind has emerged in supermarket cafés: groups of five or six young wives, having dropped their children at school except for the baby, gather for coffee, talk, and loud laughter, rather like at-least-virtuous versions of one of Alan Clark's 'covens', or groupies from an Updike novel. It sounds enjoyably confidential rather than malicious or wayward.

Inveterate working-class (and lower-middle-class) gossips could 'talk the hind-leg off a donkey', 'can't live without poking their noses into other people's business', 'gab fifteen to the dozen', 'harp on about anything under the sun', wash other people's alleged dirty linen in public.

The cardinal phrases cover most emotional possibilities: 'He's a dark horse, you know'. By now one shouldn't be surprised at the regular appearances of horses, though most of the few seen in those streets were knackered old nags drawing rag-and-bone carts. Add, just as a sample: 'the cat's out of the bag now'. I used to wonder why the cat was in the bag in the first place. Apparently some rogues at country markets used to pass-off cats in bags as sucking pigs. Hence also 'a pig in a poke'. It must have been a dumb rustic who let himself be conned in that way. More suspiciously alert was: 'he plays his cards too close to his chest'; an optional addition was, 'for comfort'. That addition meant 'for my comfort', and indicated an incipient conspiracy-theorist. One of my relatives was very fond of that phrase. To it could be added: 'You can easily read between the lines' (carried over from a form of cryptography, but who was likely to have known that?), 'she's shown her true colours now', 'there's more than one skeleton in her cupboards' (drawn from a tale about a virtuous wife, a dead husband, a rival and a duel; but not worth the carriage, as altogether too complicated and unlikely to be told in full here), 'she's swept a lot under the carpet', 'there's always wheels within wheels', and 'I don't like to tell tales out of school, but...'. It's pleasant to think that that comes all the way from William Tyndale, almost five centuries go. How rich that particular lode is.

In some restricted ways one might think of the more unpleasant kind of street gossip as filling the function of vultures swooping on garbage and consuming it in Indian cities, or that of the lowest caste of Indian society, those consigned to finding and clearing muck. On second thought, those analogies will not do. Gossips reveal, uncover, but do not remove or cleanse.

Congenital gossips have a sharp eye for faults of character and behaviour: 'She's right mean and nasty', 'don't trust him. He's all out for number one', ' as t'owd cock crows ...', 'he wouldn't even give you the skin off his rice-pudding'. Inventive, that; and it sounds home-grown. Presumably, the skin is assumed to be the part of rice pudding most easily surrendered; I always thought it the best bit. In: 'he's so tight he wouldn't give you the time of day', there is a play on double meanings, which is very unusual. Gossips, the consummate tale-bearers, could also occasionally alert the neighbours to wife- or husband-beating going on unsuspected, behind closed doors. Some of the more persistently identified victims must have 'felt their ears burning' (that occurs in Pliny and Chaucer).

In some, there had to build up a reaction to all this, a refusal to join in; not, in principle, to gossip; and a range of phrases to identify the epidemic if it reached that level: 'silence is golden', 'people in glass houses shouldn't throw stones' (that comes from at least Chaucer), 'empty vessels make the most sound', 'bad news always travels fast', 'she's not as bad as she's painted', 'give a dog a bad name' (and so justify hanging it, seems to have been the original implication), 'throw enough muck and some will stick'. These and others were useful antiseptics. For the victims themselves there was always: 'Sticks and stone may break my bones but hard words harm me never' and its   variants. The final indication of exasperated turning away could be: 'Oh Heck and Twenty'. 'Heck' is a variant of 'Hell'; but why 'Twenty'? Almost as odd, though not so difficult to trace, is 'umpteenth'. We used it to indicate a vague but large and often exasperating number or sequence—'he did that umpteen times'—and that is how it is usually defined, though an older reference describes it as a substitute for 'eleven', which makes curious another entry which dates it from 1910. Another favourite is 'Eh up!' meaning 'Steady on!' or 'Not so fast!' and sounds as though it originated as a call to horses.

Gossiping women can be funny or funny-peculiar and so sometimes figure in seaside picture postcards, along with the dread-comical, huge-bottomed mothers-in-law (who sometimes combine both roles), or for that matter a middle-aged wife herself. But they can make relations in a street turn rancid. No wonder many of the 'respectable', the equable, and the fair-minded dislike them intensely; they are often 'troublemakers'.

Quarrels

Gossip is the best seed-bed, or touch-paper, for full-scale quarrels, which can be noisy and nasty. Usually, respectable families do not engage in such bouts. They may fall-out with some neighbours, be very cool towards them or go so far as to try to ignore them. At the extreme, if relations become badly soured so that it may be said that there is 'bad blood' between them, they may even think of trying to move house.

All-out quarrels, and their concomitant 'rows', come usually from families thought to be a bit 'vulgar', loud-mouthed, not very good at looking after their children or their houses ('sluts'), sometimes with a tendency to drunkenness or even brawling, starting among themselves. As late as the nineties one quarrel could be heard screeched at full pitch on a Sunday afternoon, from the council estate over the road from us. Many of the old phrases were used but the full and free flood of obscenities, old and new, would have left my old relatives 'gobsmacked' and looking for police intervention. In the thirties we tended to expect them regularly in a street not far from us which housed a number of labouring families, descendants of the 19th-century 'navvies' (navigators, often Irish, who had toiled in digging the canals and then laying the railway lines).

Common quarrel-igniters were noisy and unruly children, accused of bullying quieter children, or of breaking windows, or petty theft. There could be regular excessive noise from a house, whether because of internal quarrels or, from the mid-thirties, radios; wind-up gramophones also appeared at about that time, but pianos and other musical instruments were rare. Today we have to add television, hi-fi's turned up too loud and staying switched on too late; and occasional electronic guitars. Surely the walls of post-war council houses are not as thin as those of back-to-backs? Otherwise, the noise levels would be almost unbearably high as well as lasting for far too long.

So 'real' quarrels went a long way beyond the fact that some neighbours just naturally 'didn't get on', saw 'eye to eye' about very little; their 'faces didn't fit', as 'oil and water don't mix' (that was one of the few that moved outside the human body for this type of image).

Sometimes we intoned that 'it takes two to make a quarrel', but that is not true of a quarrel any more than it is of a road accident. Of course, the quieter ones might have enormous resolution in refusing to be tempted to retaliate, but then they were likely to be accused of cowardice, which could at last ignite the unwilling. So it would start and escalate; the apple-cart would have been finally upset by some particularly offensive remark, and it was then time for the victim 'to read the Riot Act'. This last phrase was fairly common with us, a folk-memory from almost three centuries before.

Before long the parties were 'at it', like pot and kettle 'calling each other black', 'at daggers drawn', 'at each other's throats' (another of the body clusters), 'going off at the deep end', or 'going hammer and tongs', perhaps revealing that 'when it came to it' each could be 'as hard as nails'. The fat was well and truly 'in the fire', the 'balloon had gone up'.

As battle was engaged some epithets were obligatory and repetitive; you could have 'cut the atmosphere with a knife'. One side would be told that there was 'a bone to be picked' with the other, be ordered to 'put a spoke in it', to 'mind their p's and q's' (mild and often preambular). That is said to have been inspired by a child's difficulty in making p's and q's look different, in writing; and may be translated as: 'Tread very carefully here; we are getting near dangerous ground in this dispute'. 'Keep a civil tongue in your head' could soon be followed, as the temperature mounted, by a warning 'not to jump down my throat', or to 'rub me up the wrong way'; and soon 'the last straw' would have been added to the heightening pile.

There followed: 'keep a civil tongue in your head', 'don't try to throw that in my face' (or 'teeth'), to which the proper answer might be 'if the cap fits, wear it'. There might follow: 'don't try to put words in my mouth' or, slightly more genteel, 'save your breath to cool your broth' and, not at all genteel, 'if you don't shut up I'll give you the rough edge of my tongue'. Where does that come from? Does it hark back to a common tool such as a file or saw which had both a rough and a smoother edge? For battle to begin fully, to take off the glove, to be metaphorically and finally struck across the face, the standard phrase was: 'That's it, then...'—and off they went, firing on all cylinders (not a working-class expression). We had our own well-oiled and wide range of insults.

The onlookers had their language too, usually resigned or regretful: 'That's set the cat among the pigeons alright', 'well, they never could get along', 'they've always had a knife out for each other', 'they're paying off old scores', or 'they're making mountains out of molehills', but 'anyway, that one would cut off her nose to spite her face'.

Old Age, Ageing, and Death

'Grow old along with me'. At first glance, one might have thought that we haven't much choice, with or without Rabbi Ben Ezra, whose invitation we didn't, in Hunslet, know about anyway. He presumably meant 'grow old in the hopeful way I am doing'. That, as they say, depends. Like many of Browning's rhetorical phrases, this one is more successful as sound than in content.

A thicket of popular phrases surrounds all aspects, from the process and recognition of ageing, often belated, through to dying, burial, or cremation, and the belief in the later re-connection with the 'loved one' on the other side.

The final recognition of ageing can be, and more often than not is bound to be, sad: 'I'm getting on, you know', 'I'm beginning to feel my age', ''I'm a bit unsteady on me pins', 'I don't think I'm long for this world', 'I'm getting past it', 'sometimes I feel like nowt but skin and bone/skin and grief', 'I've one foot in the grave', 'I'm at death's door'. To all of which, a popular letting-down-gently is: 'You're not as young as you were, you know, so you need to be careful'; or the shallowly comforting: 'You're only as old as you feel, you know'.

On a second look there are in common speech at least as many cheerful or cheering-up apophthegms about the experience of old age as there are sad, such as: 'can't grumble', often followed by: 'I've had a good run' (with 'for my money,' as a fore but more often aft addition). Then, a couple of favourites because they cock a snook: 'a creaking gate hangs longest', accompanied by 'there's many a good tune played on an old fiddle', followed by 'I don't feel anything like my age'. Then: 'you're never too old to learn', which is denied by 'you can't teach an old dog new tricks' and 'there's no fool like an old fool'. The idea of a well-contented Darby and Joan— from an 18th-century ballad—still holds a firm sentimental place in many people's hearts

So does another—'myth' seems the right word—still sometimes uttered at graves and crematoria, usually after an accidental death: that the good die young. The young die in war, naturally, but here is meant more than that. It is to be found in Wordsworth: 'Oh, Sir, the good die first', which echoes Menander's 'whom the Gods love die young', and seems to linger in the depths of many people's minds, like an intolerably sad truth from far back, from an almost Greek pre-determined world—that the death of young people, however it may have come about, has a fatalistic quality. It can still haunt, on occasions.

As to the fact of death itself, there are fewer expressions. The obvious are often evasive, as in the almost universal 'passed away' in preference to 'died'. If we have at least a lingering religious feeling, we may say that the dead person has 'given up the ghost', though that is widely used by many non-religious people, as a casual, hollow image. It has perhaps been 'a blessed (or happy) release' after so much suffering; a release into 'a better world'; since our loved one is 'not lost but gone before'. Announcements in the newspapers, especially local newspapers, are rich in such euphemisms. Do many people nowadays actually expect to meet their loved ones, with full consciousness on both sides, after death? It would seem so from those still frequent tombstone inscriptions and published announcements of death, and subsequent *In Memoriams*. Hardy has a particularly and characteristically dry poem on this, apropos grief in a misguided place: 'As well weep over an unmade drain as anything else / To ease your pain'; unexpectant, stoic, qualified sympathy for others with whom you do not share that element of belief.

There are, of course, plenty of more vulgar expressions which would be unlikely to be heard in 'proper' homes but are much used in works and pubs and on the streets, chiefly among men: ' 'E's dead as a doornail' if there has, up to then, been some doubt (after an accident, perhaps); or 'he's copped it'; or 'kicked the bucket' (a memory from milking?). Some think it was taken from a word similar to 'bucket' used in certain rural areas for a beam or yoke for hanging pigs. Others think it may be taken from a common practice among suicides, though it is not used primarily to indicate that that has taken place. One of the mildest of this kind is 'he's pushing up the daisies now'.

About suicides euphemisms not surprisingly abound. They were not common, but were certainly a fairly usual fact of life in my youth. The favoured one was: 'She's done away with 'erself'; although on a closer look that is not a particularly gentle euphemism, it is kinder than 'killed herself'. 'Made an end of it' is gentler, more emollient and sympathetic, as though one can appreciate what drove her—or him, but it was usually her—to that end, an understanding of what they had had to 'go through'. Animals receive a similar, meant to be kindly, treatment: 'I think we'll have to have (the dog or cat) put down' or, even softer, 'put to sleep'.

Since, for humans, cremation is now much more frequent than burials—that is another of those surprisingly large shifts in the public consciousness compared with attitudes only half a century ago—the practice has already produced its crop of favourite judgmental epigrams. Doubts, dislike, linger. One rarely goes to a cremation without hearing someone say; 'It's not like a proper burial, is it?' Or 'It doesn't *feel* right' and 'Don't they rush and gabble through it?' 'It's a bit like one of them conveyor belts'; 'the parson was only there to earn his fee. You could see that'. A body in the earth, in a grave to be seen, prayed over by a known, local, vicar or minister, and subsequently visited and tended, still seems more in the truth.

It should not surprise us that 'death' and 'dying' occur as images all through common speech: 'If you go out like that, you'll catch your death of cold', 'I was frightened to death', ' Last time I saw

him, he looked like death warmed up', 'I will remember that to my
dying day', 'You've done that to death' (have too often uttered some
conviction or attitude or prejudice or, for that matter, sung a popular
tune), and 'He's stepping into dead men's shoes' (and the dead man
would 'turn in his grave if he knew'). We let go of such images only
with the greatest reluctance.

As to attitudes to age, ageing and dying, I have more than once
said elsewhere that lines in *King Lear* move me most, but I find
them less compelling (but not less powerful) the older I become:
'Men must endure, their going hence even as their coming hither.
Ripeness is all'. Yet that still, with Dostoevsky's Ivan Karamazov
giving back to God his entrance ticket because he will not accept a
God who creates so cruel a world, especially its cruelties towards
children; and Dylan Thomas's father being urged not to go 'gently
into that goodnight'—is the first of the three images, in descending
order of force, which do not leave me now.

*   *   *

As to class differences in the use of aphorisms, we have seen that
the large number and variety of working-class sayings about
neighbourliness have their main roots in nearness and need, which
both encourage the practice and establish its limits. Middle-class
people are more likely to have buffers of space and money between
each other. They can be 'very neighbourly' in somewhat different
senses and also practise wider friendships. The former 'working-
class' are likely still to hold to some useable old adages about
neighbourliness before they take on those of the middle class. Yet
assimilation, slowly and unsuspected but emotionally controlled assimilation, will go on.

The buffer of space can also reduce gossip and quarrels, but not
remove them. Middle-class people have their own forms and routes.
Like displaced witches, habitual working-class gossips will discover
that their usual areas for work are greatly narrowed. In the new areas
they are likely to find some different origins and so different codes
of practice. They will survive, make do, adapt, learn the new languages and targets.

Conversations in the middle class about ageing and death tend to
be more inhibited, controlled, obedient to ideas of decorum, but no
less telling within their contexts. Yet the available adages are fewer
and also less varied, less colourful, on the whole less hard and di-

rect, than in the working class, and the sentimentality has a different flavour.

About death and, in particular, about cremations, the classes are nearest to each other. Both are assimilating there what to many still, after three-quarters of a century, seems a new procedure, and conversations from different classes reveal this. Slow? At a first glance, yes; but perhaps not; that change is succeeding many centuries of graveyard burials. Here as so often the lasting power of our idioms reflects and reveals our tenacious hold on some bedrock aspects of the past.

6

Work, Class, Manners

Whether we consider the manual industry of the poor, or the intellectual exertions of the superior classes, we shall find that diligent occupation, if not criminally perverted from its purposes, is at once the instrument of virtue and the secret of happiness. Man cannot be safely trusted with a life of leisure.
—Hannah More, 'Essays'

Work

The many idioms that have over the years gathered round the idea of work fall into two main kinds. Almost all were regularly to be found before the war among the working class and some are in many people, especially men, still in use.

The more recent group, though it is already much more than a century old, comes from the overwhelming predominance of mass-industrial labour; the other recalls by contrast an older idea of crafts-manship, perhaps carried out at home or in small workshops. In those latter there could be, but was not always, a personal 'master and man' relationship and some pride, perhaps dignity, in the work done. Dickens, we always remember early, illustrated the many evils in small and sometimes large firms in the 19th century. Parts of George Eliot and other writers through to George Bourne capture something of the older-style craft relationships between master and man. Hardy stressed more the hardships of life on the land, but had an eye for honest skill.

Though work brought in bread for the family, wages might be meagre even for the skilled craftsman, and there was always the risk of being sacked if demand fell off for a particular product; especially, from about two centuries ago, through the unstoppable advance of technology. But there could also be a strong personal element in both the relations between the master and the workmen and, more deeply-rooted, between the workman and the craft he had

mastered. The first could co-exist with suspicion and even hate between the two personalities. The old adage, 'Jack is as good as his
master', had a long and sometimes violent history.

Small, boss-owned and managed firms survived and survive; there
is usually a corner —sometimes parasitic—for them to fit into and
money still to be made there. Between leaving university and being
called up I made a short journey with a man who owned a small
print works in Holbeck. This had been prompted by a newspaper
advertisement from a farmer, about fifteen miles out of Leeds, who
was seeking labour for a few weeks. The printer, probably a wid-
ower, and his adult son proved to be more or less permanent lodgers
at the farm and had been asked to give me a lift there.

From the back seat of the car I assumed there would be at least a
little conversation. I might have been an inert package they had agreed
to pick up. I half wondered why they hadn't put me in the boot. The
graceless pair in the front entirely ignored their passenger and talked
throughout of two things: the splendour of their new Wolseley car
(very upmarket in those days) in which we were riding, and matters
at the works. Their attitude was entirely money-grubbing; in pursuit
of that the men were obviously regarded as mere 'hands' who had to
be constantly watched and prodded, since they were known to be
up to all sorts of tricks and some of them, potentially if not actually,
work-shy. That was probably at least partially true; it would be interesting to know on which side the suspicions had begun. As a result,
the place was clearly run heartlessly, for as much profit as they could
squeeze from the employees. It was typical that they did not lower
their voices, or feel embarrassed that a stranger should be hearing
their unsavoury comments.

Incidentally, the farmer rejected me at once. Though he had not
said so in his advertisement, he was looking for a university student
of Agriculture, who could have given him both cheap and informed
labour. He demurred when his kinder-hearted wife suggested I be
offered a drink of tea, but finally consented to give me my bus fare
back to Leeds.

Similarly, only a few weeks before war broke out, I worked as a
labourer building sandbag shields at the wide-windowed ends of
hospital wards on the outskirts of Leeds. It was corrupt through and
through. Local officials were plainly taking back-handers to 'turn a
blind eye' to the fact that the proportions of sand to cement were
dangerously wrong. The owner's son, a local Don Juan, drove up in

a sports car from time to time and enjoyed retailing to the lads his stories of sexual conquests of receptionists at the town cinemas, and the like. The men were foolish enough to enjoy all this; he was 'a right lad' whom they admired and envied. No realisation that that right lad led his self-indulgent life on their backs. He was a small, low-level simulacrum of Lady Docker who, on a much bigger scale, lived off the workers at BSA in Birmingham; and was presented in the popular press more for the readers' enjoyment than for criticism; meanwhile, BSA foundered.

Those kinds of behaviour were on the other—less craftsmanly, more crafty—side of the 'small specialist' industries, and a strong example of the need for trade unions which, pre-war and especially in those small firms, were often not recognised. One thought of the men going out each night into those nearby mean streets to their terraced houses, not all able to take much pride in their work but well aware that 'beggars can't be choosers'. That popular adage, all the way up from the mid-15th century in various forms and tones of voice, has registered from resignation to resentment. That most such places have by now been swallowed by larger conglomerates which recognise unions, willingly or not, and have personnel officers and all the rest, can be on balance a gain.

The other range of attitudes are those brought out by the emergence of mass industry itself, the conveyor belts which in the thirties still dominated much of Leeds' labour; and were succeeded by the ever-more-complex, electronic, standardized machines for standardized work in huge units, still oddly called 'sheds', the broiler-sheds of human industry. Here, the personal connections are bound to be thinner, even though or perhaps because there may be thousands on the same shop-floor. The overriding unwritten drive is still, has to be within our system, Carlyle's 'cash nexus'; the men's personal relations, so far as they can make them, are with their 'mates'. They may hardly ever have seen the boss; their official relations are more often with the union shop stewards who usually refer to them as 'my lads', and whose main job is to protect those lads from sacking—which may now arise from decisions taken thousands of miles away.

Those are two very rough categories, but both are borne out and fleshed out by the host of routine sayings which even today are much used, not, as I said at the start, by different men but by the same individuals for different circumstances.

It seems probable that one of today's most common spare time occupations, DIY, do- it-yourself, draws on this older memory. The modern form emerged in the 1950s; *Practical Householder* started in 1958 and grew quickly. Men who have been doing much the same job with hundreds of others throughout day-after-working-day often come home and, in an entirely different spirit, settle to handiwork. They are led, obviously, by the need to get and keep the house in good shape and to save money; this is especially true of that increasing number who now 'own' (with a mortgage) their homes. But in many instances there is more than that in play.

Go round those great hangars, products of the last twenty or so years, devoted to DIY, and watch some of the men selecting materials, pulling slide-rules, spirit levels, and other gadgets out of their pockets, asking well-informed questions of the staff, and talking to like-minded men in the check-out queues about what they are engaged in, 'have in hand'—and you realise that they are drawing on a much longer tradition than that which dominates today, or probably than they meet at work or are themselves entirely conscious of. It may well have been passed on by their fathers. The paradox between the huge, echoing warehouses, many owned by global enterprises, but given to television advertisements presenting their salesmen and women as almost family friends—the paradox between all that and the old-fashioned reality of individual craftmanship as it walks those aisles—is striking.

Here a surprisingly large number of old-fashioned phrases, not all of them much used elsewhere today, come, one might say, out of the woodwork: on the need to do any job well; for a start, to 'put your back' into it (especially addressed to apprentices); to work 'with might and main' (rather earnestly biblical, that); not to 'spoil the ship for a ha'porth of tar' (sounds exactly right but some argue that it should invoke sheep not ships and refers to sheep-dipping); to 'put some elbow-grease into it, lad' (another for the apprentices; for three hundred years that has been urged on them as 'the best furniture oil'); to 'put some pride into your work'; and to 'put your best foot forward (or) foremost'. They go on, many of them admonitions to learners.

Others could just as well be addressed to lazy adults officially out of their apprenticeships, but who 'swing the lead' (surprisingly, not a naval term). 'Actions speak louder than words'; though that sounds like Protestant English it emerged in its present form from the USA;

notably, Abraham Lincoln used it. 'Put your shoulder to the wheel', 'stir your stumps', 'if a thing's worth doing, it's worth doing well', 'the devil finds work for idle hands to do' (another from that devil-bible cluster), 'practice makes perfect', but 'don't make heavy weather of it', just 'get on with it'—all those and many another make up a rich seam of traditional idioms on work-practices.

'A bad workman blames his tools' is widely taken as an accepted classic truth; we saw earlier that it had its exact counterpart in late 13th-century French. Perhaps French also contains its exasperated partner: 'If you want a thing done properly, do it yourself'. One of my relatives had a favourite image for men who failed such tests: 'He can't carry corn'. He wasn't literally expected to, either, not in those parts, but the image fitted well enough. In fact, it seemed to carry a great charge of rejection.

Mottoes such as those also recall an uncle, a modest and well-trained clerkly man, who once rightly criticised my handwriting. He had a severe, honest, and puritan attitude to the gods of skill. Over the years, whilst liking him, I acquired a strong dislike for one of his favourite epigrams: 'the labourer is worthy of his hire'. To a boss from an outsider that can sound like a proper injunction: 'pay properly'. Said by a worker it can sound cringing, as though the man is pleading with his boss to recognise and pay duly for his work, lowly creature that he is.

Another uncle advised me, in adolescence, that 'well-lathered is half-shaved'. At first, then just leaving the soft-fluff stage, I took the injunction literally. It is clearly a metaphor for 'making a good job' of everything you 'set your hand to', especially by giving it adequate preparation.

A good craftsman loves not only his tools but also his materials; he, or perhaps more likely his loyal wife, may even be willing to describe something he has made, especially if for the house, as 'a labour of love', something which has had devoted to it much more than 'a lick and a promise'. That last is an especially neat image for careless work, and recalls a cat quickly licking its paw and then, with the wet paw, wiping its face. Yet the cat's practice is probably very effective, speedy but not slack; so that application doesn't quite fit.

A good craftsman believes almost devoutly in 'every man to his trade', and that a man should always aim to 'put in a good day's work' ('for a fair day's pay', it is to be hoped). But equally: 'All

work and no play makes Jack a dull boy'. That last Jack is, surprisingly, only two and a half centuries old.

On the whole a good craftsman likes to work alone and do what
he does best: 'The cobbler should stick to his last' (that occurs in
Pliny). He rather suspects those who are 'Jacks of all trades'; and,
of course, 'masters of none'. On occasions, though, he acknowl-
edges the value of mutual help, that 'two hands are better than
one' and that 'many hands make light work'. On the other hand,
'too many cooks spoil the broth'. As so often, there are no true contradictions in that collection; each can be true, in its time and place;
there are simply different occasions for their use. If much hard work
failed to produce results, the craftsman might admit, if only to himself, that 'it hadn't panned out', which recalls painful tales of the
Klondyke.

There is a particularly likeable adage, though one not often heard:
'It's all wool and a yard wide'. In other words, it's the best stuff you
can buy, sturdy, without poor admixtures and a workable width. It
sounds as though it has come straight out of the West Riding of
Yorkshire woollen district, up in the hills near Dewsbury; or from
Huddersfield, where the best worsted came from.

It is difficult to find phrases that have a comparable role in com-
menting on modern conditions of work. One does still hear a great
many phrases loved by the unions such as that habit mentioned earlier, of referring to those, whom the bosses may know as 'the men',
as 'my lads'. Obviously, that is meant to be neither patronising nor
belittling, but does a little sound as though it refers to adolescents
who are being led by wiser heads, or like a joshing amateur football
team manager. It comes oddly from the mouth of a middle-aged,
tough negotiator, especially when he is staring across the table in
confrontation at the bosses.

By contrast, there is also that fascination with polysyllabic or pompous or abstract words, which are perhaps thought to belong to the
world of the managers and are certainly alien to the world of the
lads; they might also be thought to best suggest arguments as weighty
as the words themselves. Then there are the conventional terms of
art, packeted-phrases: 'presenting my members' fully justified demands', which are now 'put on the table', and which (until they are
negotiated) 'are categorically non-negotiable'. They are 'our final
position'; unless they are met, I will 'call for a withdrawal of labour
as at midday fourteen days hence'. Not all at Congress House nor all

at the top of some of the bigger unions still talk like that; but many do, especially shop stewards and some well above them.

A friend was the devoted chief personnel officer for one of the largest enterprises in Britain. He was a practising Christian, committed to his work, and above all anxious to do right by both men and management. What influence did he have on the top Board? Was his brief regarded up there more narrowly, less humanely, than he himself saw it? Faced with global competition, with billions at stake, and the odious rubric, 'I owe it to my shareholders' always in mind, the temper there is bound to be different; severe and calculating at best, rapacious at worst. There is bound to be continuous pressure to regard employees on the shop-floor as essentially two-dimensional units in those equations. The temper is likely to be a mixture of impersonality and confrontation, within a setting which has its own cultural-language, different from those of the men or their union officials.

Nowadays yet another element in the jig-saw is the appointment of Public Relations directors whose cardinal business, like those of Henry Wotton's diplomats, is to lie at home and abroad for their companies. That bogus 'profession', more than any other, is pushing along the current debasement of language, and expanding all the time. With few exceptions, no other work so comprehensively exemplifies the worst aspects of the consumer-and-profit-driven society. Even the advertisers usually have a real, a physical, product, against which their often excessive claims can be judged—if we are willing to take that trouble.

The powers-that-be are likely to be accused of trying to 'squeeze every ounce of work' out of the men, if possible for less money in wages; of not caring if the men are excessively hard-driven so long as they, the executives, get their production bonuses. Some executives would say a guilt-free 'yes' to that; that is the world we live in and must obey; the men have their own ways of confronting it; that's capitalism and competition. The pinnacle of that attitude today is in the grossly inflated salaries the 'fat cats' have come to expect.

The bosses say with some justification that they know the men will fiddle where they can, whether through 'knocking-off' stuff— petty theft—or in work-shirking. In Britain the night-shift at Austin's Longbridge plant used to be notorious for 'skiving'; the appalling behaviour of the old print unions is well documented. In American car plants there was, during our time there, a phrase about 'Friday afternoon cars', skimpily rushed through because men on the line were anxious to fulfil their quotas and get home without delay for the weekend (and sometimes just for the hell of it practised tricks, such as putting banana skins into gear-boxes). Have the managers found ways to discourage such practices? It is part of a continuing duel.

Yet again, unassailable as an argument to the management: 'Time is money'. To the worker: 'Time' is what you 'put in', 'go through', so as to take home a reasonably sized wage-packet. On all sides 'Time', whether as a technical term or in popular speech, appears frequently and with considerable symbolic force. Few actually say nowadays: 'Time and tide wait for no man', but old phrases such as that hover like historic warnings in the minds of both sides.

Men (and more and more women) still come home 'dog-tired' after having their 'noses to the grindstone' all day, doing repetitive tasks to a rhythm set, by new forms of technical experts, to the most productive speed for electronic machines; 'hard graft'. If someone resurrected that ancient line of talk, about 'doing an honest day's work for an honest day's pay', they would sound like missionaries; that isn't the way this world is run. They know that 'he who pays the piper calls the tune'; and that today's piper is not a colourful figure from folk festivals.

'No names, no pack-drill'. One heard that often, culled from the collective memory of army punishments—running round the bar-rack-square with full pack under the eye of a sadistic sergeant— whether for 'regulars' or conscripted men of the First World War; and now applied to loyalties of the workplace. The over-riding moral injunction on the shop-floor is to stick by your mates through think and thin; and to expect your shop stewards and the union right up to the top levels to do the same. If someone gets his cards for a serious misdemeanour, or for being work-shy, or simply and manifestly in-competent, then the men and the unions are likely to see that as justification to close ranks and if necessary to argue that black is white, and even to hint at a 'go slow', 'a walk-out' or a 'lightning strike'.

A deep dissociation has set in, set in long ago, is natural to the system. If you are a worker, you are 'at the beck and call' of the management all day, 'under their thumbs'. They 'rule the roost', are 'the big fleas' to your 'little fleas'; so you have to stand up for each other; all for one and one for all, 'come Hell or high water'; even if you know there is some human justice on the other side, such phrases are rightly still current. I once made what seemed to others a mistakenly high-minded attempt to argue for the moral as distinct from the narrowly legal aspects of a dispute. More 'realistic' opinion argued me out of such a stand.

Television can be uniquely revealing. The managing director of a range of holiday camps was shown spending a week on sites, largely unobserved and unidentified, so as to assess all aspects from the general atmosphere to the smallest practical detail. He found a lot of dissatisfaction among both clients and staff. Back at HQ he called a meeting of senior executives. Camp staff had been particularly disgruntled, almost dissident. For one thing, they resented being given dull, repetitive food much worse than that provided for the holiday makers (that was nothing to write home about, anyway). What did his colleagues propose should be done? Should the staff be given the same food as the visitors? A few guardedly sat on their hands until they had assessed the boss's inclination. One thrusting young executive, anxious to exhibit his tough credentials, argued: 'We shouldn't make any change in the staff food. It will cost too much.'

One had the impression that the M.D. had the imagination to see that, charity perhaps aside, some extra expense might be worthwhile, in bringing greater loyalty, less unpleasantness and a lower turnover among staff. Perhaps someone else at that meeting, probably getting on to the wrong band-wagon prematurely, added one of the two canonical justifications for rapacity in commerce, the one about their overriding duty to shareholders. That meeting promised to be a textbook exercise in human relations on a medium scale in modern commerce.

The greater freedom of women, in matters of sex, marriage and relations generally, is also illustrated in work. The most obvious example is in such occupations as those of check-out operators in the big supermarket chains; and the relation of that to the buying of prepared food, the funding of family holidays abroad and similar familial expenses. Less attention, at least in the daily press as distinct from specialist journals, is given to the appearance of more women in the boardroom, women who have broken through what is popularly called 'the glass ceiling'. The Office for National Statistics recently announced that there is still a long way to go before women are fairly represented. But you would need to be stubbornly, ideologically, reluctant not to note that women do appear more frequently than, say, thirty years ago as managing directors, barristers, solicitors, economic experts, broadcasting producers, and even government ministers. Simply note their appearances on television in those and other capacities. Even so far as it has gone, that change confirms that a considerable wealth of talent has been previously untapped.

Class

A common adage says: 'We are all classless nowadays'; but that is a myth. The sense of division, of separation, runs through virtually all the important interstices of our social life, is so much intertwined with our assumptions about rank, profession or work, marriage, land, money, sport and recreation, including holidays, shopping and much else, as to be invisible to many. One cannot easily look through our permanently foggy cultural climate, since it has been there for as long as can be remembered. The sense of apartness is dominant, not altogether consciously—often quite unconsciously—in many people from the securer middle class right up to those who think of themselves as in the upper reaches.

It is conscious enough in, say, that very small group of clubs (not, for instance, such as the Reform), mainly for men, most near St. James and Pall Mall, which only admit real toffs to membership. Their members still live on an upper level to which the idea of equality has hardly penetrated; they are right in that since, so far as they can see, looking out from the enclosed world they inhabit, few things have indeed changed. There are always plenty of people willing to adopt the stances of subservience, opening doors with a deferential inclination of the head, remembering names, ready to wear a sub-Ruritanian uniform, to sprinkle around many 'Sirs'; and ready for many tips. If you 'come across'—I use that phrase in preference to 'meet', for obvious reasons—there certainly could be no meeting of minds with that branch of the 'upper crust'. It is almost shocking to realise how untouched for at least three centuries their daily club life has been, how inviolate it can still seem. Along with land, a 'name' on the Stock Exchange, the right school and accent, and perhaps a safe Conservative seat, this form of belonging will be one of the last accoutrements of which they will let go. Few are greatly pushing them in that direction.

In vastly different but related ways, working-class people were before the war conscious of class divisions all the time. That heavily weighted word 'respectable' is used so much because it suggests a different scale of values from that of social class. Its opposite is 'common as muck'. One greatly hated word was 'snubbed', meaning obviously treated as of a lower order.

That sense is still there though to some extent muted, especially because commodity-driven consumerism must regard all as equal not just before the law—that is a proper democratic principle—but before the shop-tills. That can lead to the false principle of head-counting; levelling. As a consumer, Jack is certainly as good as his master, whether consuming goods or opinions or prejudices even when those may be meretricious, so long as profits continue to rise. So today many, especially young people, are led to feel equal in false terms; they are less aware, hardly at all aware, of a new social pyramid which for many of them is as limiting as the old, but is by now hidden under the sound of insistent youth entertainment: music, beer, celebrity-gawping, sex. This reduces any inclination to examine the true but hidden constraints on their lives

For those who have been at 'Public' and other private schools, the sense of class-division is, behind all the bland protestations, still generally alive. To maintain that sense and its presumed concomitant advantages is still, whether admitted or not, one of the purposes of most of those schools; or many parents would not think them worth their fees. 'Class' and its relevant manners are then more than a sort of badge, though they are certainly that. They are passports to good opportunities, to the right kinds of profession and groupings. It must be cosy inside there, especially warmed by the feeling that most others are well outside.

Older attitudes towards classes above us were, as were so many parts of our lives, divided. On the one hand, much was accepted, especially if it was a bit raunchy as in some aristocratic behaviour. Auden's image of the upper class and the working class meeting at horse-races and leaving the middle class, the grey hole in the middle, to look after the shop, comes to mind again. It has, though, the excessive neatness of many a striking contrast. I saw it illustrated, though, in the ways of a retired miner; he had a touch of raffishness which went well with his betting on the 'gee-gees'. Working-class people who joined the nobs at the races were particularly alien to our kind.

There could also be deference to titles, especially when hereditary, and much enjoyment in gossip about them. We did not want to

mix, even if we had had the opportunity; we preferred our aristocrats to be separate, a bit exotic and so available for tale-telling from
time to time, especially if that was salacious. The Lascelles at
Harewood House, a few miles out of Leeds were, before the war,
'looked up to' by many in the working and lower middle classes.
They were also the source of much scandalous gossip. Did the Lord
really beat his wife, a member of the Royal family? Was one of the
sons going out with a girl from a well-to-do North Leeds Jewish
family? Was there a confidential meeting, with lawyers in attendance,
in the lounge of the Queen's Hotel, City Square, to engineer a solution to so undesirable a connection? That thirties lounge was the
perfect setting for such a meeting: ostentatiously fussy, louche,
arriviste.

That particular kind of deference is less obvious today. We still
need people if not quite 'to look up to' then certainly for our raw,
levelling gossip. So we have the ever-increasing cult of the 'celebrity' which had its most recent apogee in the astonishingly inflated
figure of Princess Diana, and now runs through best-selling authors,
footballers, pop-stars to what it is fashionable to call the 'D-List', the
most ephemeral. To a BBC reporter, a scandalous 'celebrity' trial
was 'one of the most important the Old Bailey has ever seen'. No
historical sense there. Now religion has almost gone and aristocracy
no longer counts for much, we are left with a swirling rag-bag; one
of the saddest phenomena of this 'democratic' age. We had some
respect for the Methodist minister, the doctor, and the Church of
England vicar, in ascending order; but we knew the minister was the
most approachable by people such as us. Catholic priests belonged
to another caste, virtually untouchable and not easily comprehended.

Above all, we liked to think that we could recognise 'real style'
when it appeared, and knew how to give it 'its due'. Not so to the
self-made man, unless he wore his wealth lightly. Land and an inherited title still counted for much more. But the Hoggarts, as has
been already made abundantly clear, were similar to a large proportion in our streets, respectable working class; and, if we had both-
ered to vote, would have perhaps been deferential Conservatives.
Certainly, we had on occasions our own kinds of snobbery.

Top-drawer academic life was in a class of its own. Professors
were remote figures, to be viewed with some awe, the title itself
strangely impressive. We had all met doctors and parsons; few of us
had ever seen a professor. One of my aunts, explaining my accent to

her neighbours (it is still recognisably Northern, but was not to her; she heard above all the non-Northern differences), settled for: 'Doesn't he talk just like a doctor?' The respect given to a professor was not inspired only by respect for social status, but as much by a touch of deference still to the idea of learning, of what seemed to them an other-worldly, an academic, life. In that respect the University up past the Civic Hall was a most impressive institution whose premises hardly any of us expected ever to enter.

A curious habit illustrates where social and academic snobbery could come together in the provinces. Leeds University was and is by international standards a distinguished institution. The private Leeds Grammar School just next to it was notoriously snobbish in the typical provincial-professional way. Tony Harrison writes of being allowed only to play the drunken porter in *Macbeth* because of his deplorable Leeds working-class accent. That raises the amusing thought of the Scottish King uttering his great speeches in Roundhay's unmistakably Northern, provincial-middle-class accents.

Some of that school's pupils were coached in the hope of Oxbridge entrances; but the school's solid central job was to educate to a certain level the children of the Leeds professional or near-professional classes who would pay, from doctors to estate-agents. Even after the war, some masters there, anxious to give a push to lagging students, would warn them that if they didn't do better they wouldn't have a chance of Oxbridge and, dire fate, would have to settle for 'that place up the road'. This was not an academic nor indeed an intelligent judgment, but a snobbish, narrow, low-level provincial, social class threat. A letter of rebuke from 'The Senior Management Team' there, sent recently to a former pupil and now famous writer (no; not Tony Harrison this time) who had criticised the school, suggests that the old spirit lives on, except for acquiring something of PR management-speak.

A recent proud remark by a senior academic about his wife's renown perfectly catches the English habit of making class-divisions everywhere: 'She had honorary degrees from major universities'. Had she refused degrees from what he would call 'minor universities', or did he think them not worth acknowledging?

More evidently than a little awe before some of those 'above us', there could of course be resentment. The most frequently employed single expression which indicated the resentment divide was: 'Them and Us'; much fell into one or other of those compartments. 'They' were down in the Town Hall, running things, or up in the posher districts such as Roundhay, 'pulling strings', 'having things all their own way'; 'money talks'; we got 'the mucky end of the stick'; we expected little from 'Them'.

In the early 1990s I was filming aspects of Leeds for television. This included long shots of some of the grander roads of Roundhay. An expensively dressed woman in early-middle-age strode out from her garden-gate and demanded to know, in the most haughty and imperious tones, what we thought we were doing in photographing her house. Her whole manner was so insulting, so *de haut en bas,* so lacking in anything approaching good manners, that it would have been difficult to reply civilly. The producer took over and adopted his well-practised professional mollifying style. The woman merely strode back to the house without a word, ill-mannered throughout. It was intriguing to guess her background. She did not look or sound like 'new money'; perhaps, rather, like the wife of a managing director or very senior surgeon.

Class-feeling among us could be one-sided and mean, but it indicated how little change most of us expected. We could be unjust, in the thirties, to the Leeds Housing Authority which, though like many others it made mistakes, did not customarily act as though it was doling-out charity; it was clearly 'on our side'. This was partly due to a socialist Church of England vicar who was also a councillor. One articulate and passionate member such as that can make a vital difference. The City Libraries Committee built in the middle thirties, when the slump still held, a good library in the heart of Hunslet, which helped transform the lives of many of us. The City Education Committee could be unbureaucratically generous to bright kids who needed a leg-up.

Those were official matters; already in some areas such as local government people were becoming aware that local democracy ought to mean fewer divisive attitudes and hierarchies. Elsewhere in many parts of our lives we had learned, and continued to be resentful, to cock a snook or be bloody-minded, to reject the 'piss-proud' (not our house's language but so vivid as to be worth introducing at least once) person who made us exclaim: 'Who does he think he is?', to assert that 'a cat may look at a King', that 'fine feathers don't make fine birds'; that, though we were 'not born with silver spoons in our mouths', we knew how to 'behave properly'. That signified, above all, not being uppish towards others; we had had enough of that directed at us. 'Manners', learning how to behave whatever your position on the social ranking-scale, were one of the best and most varied indicators of the reaction against the meaner operations of the class-sense; and deserve a section of their own, immediately following this.

An interesting and crowded branch-line here leads, again as so often, straight to the ways in which idioms can indicate class differences and assumptions in varying situations. This was played around with, to some extent, in the 'U' and 'non-U' arguments of about forty years ago. Ironically, those were inspired not in a scholarly journal by an Oxbridge don, but by the later 'vulgarising' (in the favourable French sense) of an article first published in such a journal and written by a devoted scholar—at Leeds University.

Betjeman played happily with those differences also, though chiefly at the frontiers where the more genteel edges of lower-middle-class and middle-class life meet the frontier of the confident upper-middles. Some of the differences between working-class and middle-class locutions for specific activities have already been noted, particularly in the section on Drink; there are many more. We almost all have our built-in, instantaneously active as needed, mental machinery for making these distinctions according to our sense of our own place, or would-be place. Those who most vociferously assert that the fact and the sense of class have virtually disappeared often do so in ways which implicitly indicate the opposite. The louder the protester, the greater the impercipience.

Manners

It is surprising now to remember how often the concept of 'good manners' appeared in pre-war working-class speech, especially among the 'respectable'. Like cleanliness, it was something one held firmly on to, which indicated that you were not of the lowest lower-order, that you knew how to behave, perhaps especially 'in company'. It was a defining rod that helped you to grade people, especially those who might think themselves 'better than you'; socially at least, morals rarely came consciously into the count but were often there at the back. It should not need saying that the rules for relationships here could be different from but no less complex than those of other classes.

Not surprisingly, one of their central principles—perhaps the most central—was and is anti-snobbery itself, the rejection of those who 'give themselves airs', who 'stick their noses in the air', who 'get above themselves', who 'play the Big I Am', who assume superiority in status, money, style, in the fact that they have more to spend on clothes than those around them, or have had a slightly better education and acquired what they believe to be better forms of speech; or have better houses, children at a private school, a bigger car, more expensive holidays each year; in short, people who act like 'little tin gods' by displaying many forms of unwarranted vanity. That selective bundle includes unattractive behaviour from some very respectable working-class and some lower-middle-class people; and a few from middle-class encounters. Such people, if of your own kind, are disliked even more than the others; neighbours know well how to bring down a peg or two those who are physically and socially nearer to themselves.

Clearly the range of aphorisms centred on such people whose whole manner suggests that they have too high an opinion of themselves, is long and deep-seated. They were 'stuck up', 'too big for their boots', acting like 'his nibs', 'giving themselves too many airs and graces', 'toffee-nosed and probably no better than they should be'. They 'go with themselves'—a fine image used in our house only by that aunt who had an ear for language. It conjures up the picture of a person so proud that they carry round with themselves an invisible *claque* or set of clapping clones.

The group of epigrams based chiefly on appearances are on the whole a cheerful lot: 'She's all dressed up and nowhere to go'; 'he looks like the dog's dinner' or 'like something the cat's brought in'; she—or he—is 'dressed up to the nine's' (to perfection—and found in Robert Burns and many others later), is 'dressed to kill', 'showing off'', pretending to be a toff. More hurtfully, she's 'mutton dressed as lamb'; and more vulgarly, 'she's all fur coat and no knickers'. More primly: 'Beauty is only skin deep'.

Many of the above were frequently heard in the Hoggart household. I do not think they were inspired by simple jealousy, but rather by the old puritan distrust of excessive display. One may enjoy 'dressing up'; it is the flaunting to which objection is taken. Objected to if found in 'your own' (relatives) even more; on such occasions there entered a mixture of mockery of them and self-mockery. As to visitors, 'dressing up' to receive them was alright so long as it was not ostentatious: ' I'd better put on my best bib and tucker if *they're* coming', my 'glad rags', 'my Sunday best'.

Many other phrases in this area of manners carried moral or near-moral judgments: 'Handsome is as handsome does', 'it costs nothing to keep a civil tongue in your head', 'politeness costs nothing', 'I'd be grateful if you'd mind your manners more' (these often in response to the feeling that the person concerned is being impolite to them because they are assumed to be inferior); 'every cock crows on its own dungheap (all the way from Seneca), and a really sarcastic put-down which reverses roles: 'I see it's no use casting pearls before swine'.

There comes to mind at this point, and by contrast, a favoured Northern working-class form of polite farewell: 'Well, I'll love you and leave you'. That is very likeable and gentle, compared with the locutions above, most of which are comical or dismissive reactions to something which has understandably been taken amiss. Similarly, 'You look real smart in that'—a new dress or suit—is straightforward praise. 'Oh no! that scarf! It *doesn't go* with that dress' is a death sentence on the scarf. But there is admiration for particularly attractive physical qualities: 'She's a lovely-looking lass', or 'he's a fine-looking lad—nice, too, and very well-mannered'. Psychologically, such a one would rank along with the 'real ladies and gents', with those who had no 'side', however well-to-do or well-bred they were.

One young working-class man of whom such remarks were made was exceptionally 'well-spoken' and 'well-mannered'. We learned later that he was not long out of Borstal, where he had been 'taught manners'. Not much afterwards he went back to jail for four years, for hitting a taxi-driver with a half-brick instead of paying his fare.

Retribution was hinted at in the worst cases, as in: 'He'll have to eat humble pie before he's much older'. That is usually taken in the standard modern adjectival sense of 'humble'. Apparently it derives from 'umble' (dictionaries do say that this antique word did of course change into our 'humble'). That was the name, noun, for the entrails and offal of the deer, which was cooked for the lower orders, the huntsmen; venison pie was for the gentry at the top table. In the English language, you can hardly ever get away from 'class'.

After that, the naval-flag derivation of 'he needs taking down a peg or two' sounds almost classless, as do 'pride always comes before a fall', and 'but anyway, he's his own worst enemy', which sounds sensibly understanding.

Set against such people as the above are those who 'hide their light under a bushel', who 'never push themselves forward' but are 'content to take a back seat', or who are 'rough diamonds' but 'the salt of the earth'—'when it comes down to it'. The Bible is often hovering in the background, with its bushels and salt and yokes and tares; and its prophecies such as 'the last shall be first and the first last', and the most notable guest at the foot of the table. But perhaps only there until spotted and called forward again. Does the entirely un-notable guest, who had been mistakenly led up there, then go back to the bottom? You never know, in England.

*   *   *

Globalisation has not so far made irrelevant most aphorisms—almost all unpleasant—about work and the bosses. They will last unless and until capitalism's natural impulses are better reined in than seems likely at present.

Insofar as it remains, the sense of individual craftsmanship will be more and more enclosed in the world of Do It Yourself, provision for which is now, ironically, as we have seen, being made on a global scale.

Idioms that express class-divisions are in a paradoxical condition. Those which carry the sense of old-style divisions are less used, as mass public voices increasingly insist that we are all equal nowadays. That myth has yet to produce many of its own satirical counter-images. So far not enough people have seen through that false pattern and its promises.

To the extent that the upholding of 'good manners' was bound up with the preservation of old-style working-class self-respect, itself often a reaction against a lack of respect from those above, is also being made to seem increasingly irrelevant. If it is to last, the concept of 'good manners' will need to find a further and firmer foothold; to shed itself of any hint of deference; to recognise that social conditions and manners which once seemed impregnable or at least unchangeable are indeed changing; but to recognise also that some changes are towards false horizons.

7

Language and Vulgarity:
The Life of the Mind

*You taught me language; and my profit on't
Is, I know how to curse.*
                                    —The Tempest

The Rude and the Obscene

'Vulgarity, blunt speaking, evasion, and its handmaiden euphemism' could have been a more comprehensive if over-wordy title for the first part of this chapter. Blunt speaking often moves towards the vulgar, but may be justified and accepted so long as it doesn't explicitly step over the normally accepted boundary. Evasion and euphemism are extremely favoured ways of avoiding the other two; and have their own special ways of indicating but avoiding those threatening excesses, especially where vulgarity threatens to move into the obscene. We used to say that speaking in such a vulgar manner was to be 'a bit off colour'. A delicate cop-out. Reference books tend to place that as first appearing during the 1950s. It was in use by us in the thirties. Perhaps the related abbreviation—'a bit off'—came in after the last war. Or perhaps the two had long coexisted, one a very slightly more sophisticated form.

Such delicacies were applied fairly often so as to avoid folk-phrases which called 'a spade a spade' or, even less agreeable, 'a bloody shovel'; phrases which—especially as to sexual matters—did not mince words. Most of us knew some of those sayings by adolescence, but did not bring them into the house.

Each class, each sub-division of class, had its own proscribed areas. People with first-generation English, no matter how sophisticated they were, had (and have) to be particularly sensitive, aurally, if they are not to commit linguistic oddities. A friend and his wife

were both members of intellectual Central European Jewish families. They had escaped from Hitler in the mid-thirties and arrived in
time to enter distinguished independent grammar schools. In most
circumstances their English seemed faultless and they had both acquired consummately Oxford accents. We were at dinner with them
one evening when it became clear that their little boy was clutching
his crutch.

According to class and education some mothers might have asked:
'Do you want to go to the bathroom/ toilet/lavatory/loo'? or 'Do you
want to wee/wee-wee/do number one?' Some of us, being 'liberated', might have asked: 'Do you want to pee?'. There, the mother
asked: 'Do you want to piss?'. There was a very slight tremor in the
room. Horses piss and rough workmen announce: 'I need a piss.'
Even most liberated English intellectuals would at that time have
been unlikely to use such a word in company. The mother's ear had
let her down there; or perhaps she knew perfectly well that that was
a vulgar form and didn't mind—being an even more effectively liberated intellectual than most of her guests.

Many working-class people wished to keep clear of those who
were 'common'. 'Common as muck' was the hardest dismissal.
'Common as the hedge' is a milder old form, but seems not to have
been widely adopted; there, the rural memory did not carry over.
Phrases such as 'the common touch' and, even more surely, 'the
light of common day' belong to an altogether more assured and kind-
lier world of discourse. Still, resolutely respectable working-class
people were well practised in multiple evasion-by-euphemism as
they avoided vulgar speech. We made most frequent use of the direct workaday rebuff: 'don't use bad language here', or 'that's too
near the knuckle', and the inevitable military image: 'He swears like
a trooper', which comes from well before this century's wars.

'Bottom' was never 'bum' in our house. Breasts were spoken of
in the safely singular, as 'bust' or 'bosom'. Some referred to 'the
bosom' in a manner which suggested that they had almost entirely
escaped from the admission that there were after all two of those
things; that would have been publicly recognising too much about a
private part of the female body. Lads in the street preferred 'tits'
(three or four centuries old) and, more recently, 'knockers' (which
came before the war from the USA) or 'Bristols', though that interchangeable rhyming slang (Bristol City = Titty, or Birmingham City,
or...) was slightly socially superior and probably post-Second World

War. In Copenhagen shop-windows, I noticed with pleasure, the brassiere seemed to be called a 'bust-holder-up' or 'upholder'; singular again, but one can hardly be more exact than that.

'Cunt' was the most common of its kind and has the most complex and long etymology; it was followed by 'fanny' (its genealogy is in dispute. Eric Partridge related it to Cleland's *Fanny Hill* of 1749, but understandably that hasn't been widely accepted). The most unpleasant sounding was 'twat', which may derive from a dialect word for a 'narrow passage'; it was readily joined with several adjectives to make a number of favoured combinations ('you fucking twat'), all equally unpleasant.

Indoors, the phrase 'down there' indicated a swathe from below the navel to just above the knees. We could not have said 'nude' or hardly 'naked'; and 'in the buff' was not in our lexicon. It occurs in at least the mid-17th century, and in Mayhew in the mid-19th century he described 'a fine young chap' working hard 'stript to the buff'. It does not follow that the London workman would himself have used the phrase any more than we did. 'Not a stitch on' expressed a domesticated medium degree of shock, but 'in their birthday suits' was primly quite acceptable, so long as it referred only to children, especially pre-pubescent girls. 'Chamber-pot' could cause slight embarrassment and led to what-the-hell vulgarisms on the left hand, such as 'piss-pot', and foggier and foggier euphemisms on the right. The gentility trail led from 'chamber pot' to 'pot' to 'article' to the sinister 'thing'.

Back in the street, 'arse' (4th century) and 'shit' (has a long history in various forms) were simply part of the everyday group: 'shit or bust' as you took a risk, 'he doesn't know his arse from his elbow', 'he's a pain in the arse', and 'I went arse over tit' (fell right-over). All such were not fully domesticated and most people took the easiest way out when searching for strong but just useable images; they avoided those frontier examples. By contrast, 'policemen don't shit roses', though it would not have been acceptable in our house, had the authentic ring of hard experience. It is difficult to find in print. One would not expect to find it in earlier editions of Brewer (the first edition was in 1870); that and some of its successor editions are implacably sanitised, like the pre-trial editions of *Lady Chatterley's Lover.*

Predictably, all aspects of sex, whether in themselves natural and not—except by the incorrigibly prudish regarded as obscene—were linguistically evaded almost as much as the manifestly obscene (as they were in almost all other parts of society except, apparently, some of the aristocracy). Their use of the phrase 'in pig' for being pregnant has already been noted. Of the earth, earthy; that; and partner to the more domestic rather than farm-yard image favoured by some working-class people: 'a bun in the oven'; except that that would be thought vulgar by most in that class whereas the aristocrats' form could apparently be used across their class with no inhibition. We last heard it in 1974, from the Countess already mentioned. It did, however, slightly sound as though it was a naughty phrase remembered from her Young Ladies College.

With us, 'in the family way' was also thought a bit gamey. Obviously, 'in trouble' was a different thing altogether, its meaning clear and sadly honest by its own lights; of a young woman it could not mean that she had committed a slight misdemeanour at work. 'In the pudding club' was downright vulgar, slightly below but metaphorically related to having something in the oven. 'Being ruined' belonged to the Music-Halls and, later, Miss Otis.

There were very fine discriminations here. In our house someone might just have said 'in the family way', accepting the very slight gameiness (source books tend to enter this as 'pregnant—informal', which conjures up some pleasant misinterpretations), but we would not even have talked of having 'a bun in the oven' and even less of someone being 'up the spout'. Yet the relative who, after a bad first pregnancy, said she never wanted to go through that again, was straightforwardly told: 'Nay, they don't oppen t'oven door for one loaf'. That belonged to acceptable folk wisdom not urban prurience and was said by one still in touch with her rural background. That whole idiom—'bun in the oven'—is not easy to find in print, though both 'bun' and 'oven' are slang words for the pudendum. Perhaps it died out with that old woman's generation. Or perhaps it lingers, as certainly does its obverse, among some of the old and very respectable. A book of mine, which talked of some of these vulgar phrases, was kept from an elderly aunt as being too shocking to read.

It is joined by 'a slice off a cut loaf is never missed', which is more 'wink-wink' in character, knowing, as if it has come out of the mouth of a city spiv. It sounds even of the 20th century and the supermarket sliced loaf. It appears in *Titus Andronicus*; but, like most of its other occurrences, it may have there a larger reference than the merely sexual. A less flippant variation is: 'what the eye doesn't see, the heart doesn't miss'.

We are back with the cruder kind in: 'Yer don't shit on your own doorstep', which, too, could have wider meanings but which I first heard a man use when explaining why he had 'refused the advances' (scandalised popular Sunday newspaper language) of his landlady's daughter in Rochester; her husband was at sea. The world of the smutty picture-postcard again. If the landlady's daughter is 'no beauty' then that need not be a bar to accepting her offer. After all, 'Yer don't look at the mantelpiece when yer poke the fire'.

There is a slightly sophisticated street joke that may have been invented by a wit further up and passed down, but which was enjoyed by some of the more self-conscious adolescents of our area. A beautiful and expensively dressed young woman gets out of a fine motor car in a working-class street and goes into a house. A group of boys playing there stare at her, wondering who she is. One of them says: 'Oh, that's only our Edna; she's gone wrong'.

The euphemisms for the act itself, for 'having sex', which is itself today's favourite and weak evasion, are a desperate, tatty lot. Even though 'fuck' can be printed almost anywhere now, most of us reserve it for the occasions when it is logically, for the sake of the argument, unavoidable. To use it in public might still offend some people or be seen as a touch of showing-off, and would usually not add much to understanding.

There are a good few genteel evasions and a host of less genteel. In any dictionary of Slang, they are likely to occupy several closely printed pages, and eventually a reading produces the same effect as a cheap, soft-porn film, limply rolling past. Most belong also to the world where we use a French word for a contraceptive sheath, and the French return the non-compliment.

Others, in the sexual area, range from the racy, such as to 'roger' or to 'get a leg over' or to have a 'knee-trembler'; that last slightly surprisingly, since it was a favourite phrase among Hunslet adolescents when a girl let them 'go part of the way', comes from more than a century ago. From there to the less explicit, extremely evasive but still usually intelligible: 'having a bit of hanky-panky', or 'a bit of slap and tickle'; and so back again to 'going the whole way' and 'having a bit on the side'.

We do badly need a straightforward word, if only because 'went to bed with' is such a silly euphemism, as is 'slept with' which means the opposite of what it says. 'Made love' is too tender for some occasions and should be kept for specifically more tender experiences. 'Copulation?'—ugh! 'Coition', 'coitus', 'fornication', 'sexual intercourse'. The line rolls on and on until one begins to feel like falling back on 'fuck' again.

Only two street-words for masturbate come to mind: to 'toss yourself off', which has the merit of metaphoric precision, and to 'wank'. There must have been others, perhaps many; but we appear to have largely made do with those two. Other common expressions lived in the escapist clouds: 'No better than she should be' instead of 'she's a loose woman', that being a harsher because more direct form; and one which came through a rather proper woman's pursed lips: 'Oh, he's one of those who is *not interested in women, you know*'.

Straightforwardly blunt, direct speaking as distinct from the truly vulgar varies from the long-recalled folksy to the often muckily urban. The best, new or old, are down-to-earth, shrewd, occasionally sardonic, straightforward but not straight-laced, often pin-pointing hard lessons in life, and witty. Even the vulgarly urban, such as that about policemen quoted above, are often worth their continued passage because they have some of those qualities.

Such phrases, not necessarily vulgar, but always telling, bob up, are pressed into service like universal currency, in all aspects of life. Many of them have been quoted here already and more will be. Some appear again here, put together now to illustrate their common qualities, another family group to which they belong.

'Better the day, better the deed'; that has a crisp, no nonsense Protestantism. From the early 14th century, it has usually been employed to justify working on a Sunday and so, that argument having been decided, might seem no longer necessary today. We seemed not to relate it to the Sabbath but rather employed it to suggest almost the opposite: that things done on a happy—cheerful, sunny—day ('a real day off') are likely to be well done. 'Little things please little minds' belongs to that group and appears in Ovid's *Ars Amatoria*. Apparently it was once used as a motto in a Galt Toys catalogue, which clearly misapplied it. Modern adspeak is not strong on ironic, hard or judgmental language.

'If the cap fits, wear it', 'as plain as the nose on my face'; that intriguing 'all my eye and Betty Martin', 'tell that to the Marines' (Charles II, showing incredulity), 'let's get down to brass tacks' (19th century American into Hunslet), and—one of the popular devil-cluster—'tell the truth and shame the devil', 'a fool and his money are soon parted', and 'he's got more money than sense'—all those can stand for several others of the blunt, straight-up-and-down sort. An oddity is 'without rhyme or reason'—one of those drawn from contexts (such as, here, mid-17th-century educated French) which most speakers may never have inhabited, such as the practice of rhyming or logic—which is picked up and carried along because it hits the mark, to describe something which makes no sense at all.

Then a bunch that warn off and so join some of those advices to caution so frequent in the working class and often picked up from other sources or classes because they fit: 'Don't play with fire', 'don't skate on thin ice', 'curiosity killed the cat'. Particularly curious, hard-nosed with its casual threat (and tougher than 'to argue with the gloves off') is: 'a cat in gloves catches no mice', which appears in the mid-15th-century Towneley Play of Noah, but never got as far as Hunslet. Several such pertinent, pleasant and often hard-nosed sayings were also not picked up by us, no doubt for a variety of reasons. Others continue to live: 'ask no questions, hear no lies.' Seeing is believing', 'many a true word is spoken in jest', 'a nod is as good as a wink to a blind horse' (used to indicate either futility or quickness in the uptake), and 'what the eye doesn't see, the heart doesn't grieve', 'a wise child knows its own father', 'hard words break no bones' and, in more than one sense, 'any port in a storm'. In those last few, realism, down-to-earthiness, even cynicism predominate. Of which one of the least acceptable domestically, but most effective in its vulgarity, is: 'Well, bugger that for a lark'. More polite versions are: 'Stuff that for...'; or 'Sod that for a game of soldiers'; and the most vulgar is 'Fuck that for...'.

Finally, about the current alterations in sexual frankness. One clear change among many people in the last few decades (perhaps since the *Lady Chatterley's Lover* acquittal) has been the greater readiness to speak, listen to, read and write sexually vulgar language. Television is a good indicator. From the day when Kenneth Tynan said 'fuck' there, the habit has spread, stopping only—so far—at the really nastily vulgar words such as 'cunt' and 'twat'. Of course, these limited changes have at the moment stopped before reaching the respectable working class and upward; of the older generation, that is (except, as we saw much earlier, for at least one senior civil servant and one Oxbridge College chaplain). In this, as in some other matters, the habits of younger people are affected more by peer groups than by the sense of where they fit socially.

Intelligence, Intellect, and Imagination

It is a commonplace, and true, that the English publicly and often individually seem not to value 'the life of the mind' very highly, as compared with, for instance, the French. In the acts and symbols of public life that is true. To some degree, Matthew Arnold's three-part division of the population—Barbarians, Philistines, and Populace— still has a little force, especially at the upper-class end. We have no Academy, and do not much care officially what happens to our language; nor do we publicly as much honour our artists, writers, thinkers as the French do; and our national educational systems tend to give people distinguished in such ways a lower place than is given to the Monarchy, the Empire, wars, great soldiers and statesmen/politicians (we also neglect, in telling our history, the lives of the majority, of the working people). We see ourselves as more relaxed, informal, demotic and so tend to be rather scornful of what we see as the rigidly logical, often centralised and more formalistic French systems in many parts of their society.

In fact we are often Gradgrinds; vocationally, not imaginatively, minded. We live in the native country of a supreme literary mind, one recognised virtually all over the world; but some of our present examining boards are so crass as to wish to delete Shakespeare from the school's syllabus on the ground that he is not 'relevant'. The Base Indians, the semantically stone-deaf, in action.

We do tend to admire intelligence; we have some internationally respected institutions of higher education and often point out, rightly, that we collect at least, if not more than, our 'share' of Nobel prize-winners, according to size of population. We can be inventive and untrammelled in the free range of our intelligences. All that is true, too.

So: intelligence, yes, and of the highest order. But here we are looking at something else, at our *attitudes* toward two other qualities: the intellect (as compared with intelligence) and the imagination. Can intellect and imagination really be separated? They seem to work together; but can they be distinguished from intelligence? An intelligence can operate without an interest in ideas in themselves, ideas for their own sake but which cannot in the end, some of us still tend to hope, be thus separated from questions of value.

Yet a superb intelligence may be able to become chess champion of the world, or create a most complex computer, or crack an immensely sophisticated code, or successfully build the highest skyscraper ever, or create a new and horrendous bomb. It may carry out those and many like activities without ever stepping outside them and asking questions about 'to what good end' they might or should be used.

The life of the intellect does step outside. Its guiding motto, inevitably quoted repeatedly, is Socrates': 'the unexamined life is not worth living'. Equally inevitably, someone—an intellectual—will go on to say: 'Better a human being dissatisfied than a pig satisfied.' An intellectual asks not only 'how' but 'why' all the time; questions life in all its aspects, but especially asks about the worthwhileness of the way it is being lived, or endured, whether by himself or herself or other individuals or whole societies. Intellectual enquiry is therefore likely to be suspected by many forms of government; though on the whole is tolerated by forms of would-be democracy such as ours. But the fact that the intellectual mind is intrigued by questions of value, moral questions, ethical questions, does not necessarily mean that it allows itself to be guided by them; that would be too easy a conjunction. A celebrated philosopher gave a lecture at Birmingham, brilliantly. Leaving at the end, one of his colleagues observed, laconically, that in his personal life he was a swine. Obviously, there need be no connection; but many of us go on assuming or at the least wishing that there might be; and that that connection might lead to better choices being made.

Are highly intelligent people also intellectuals or imaginative or both? Some are, certainly, and many a scientist will argue strongly that to make great advances in their disciplines requires 'a leap of the imagination'. But why shouldn't it be called 'a leap of the intelligence', without denying that such a person might well have intellectual and imaginative powers? Unless the words are going to be rather simply run together wouldn't we gain from trying better to distinguish intelligence from intellect; and perhaps, which is harder, intellect from imagination?

Literary people tend to call in aid here Coleridge at his most marmoreal: 'The primary imagination I hold to be the living power and prime agent of all human perception and as a repetition in the finite mind of the eternal act of creation in the infinite I AM'. It is hard fully to understand all that but its confidence is immensely impressive as is its belief in 'the eternal act of creation'. There are predictably very many philosophical and conflicting studies of 'imagination' from many centuries and countries. Direct experience of people known, especially in early life, and at that time among one almost compacted and 'lower' social group, led me to attempt to tease at how 'intelligence', 'intellect', and' 'imagination', showed themselves there and then; and also how they were generally regarded, especially as—to stick to the thread of this book—they expressed themselves in usual speech, above all in that working class.

In our part of Leeds in the thirties, there were many intelligent people around us, people whose intelligence was not greatly nourished at school. Some teachers would recognise them and try to 'bring them on'; others—we had in my elementary school a prime example—were teachers who assumed that they were in a 'dump' district, one in which the kids were in their view almost all rather stupid, and 'taught' them accordingly. The never-ending revolving of low expectations, again; the widespread waste again. Of course, some were not well-endowed, nor were or are some in those Private Comprehensives we call Public Schools. If the brighter ones among us also had some 'push' or 'drive' about them, they could with or without help from a teacher 'get on' within their area, its activities and opportunities, and become local entrepreneurs; or they could push further afield. They would pull themselves out. The most important first point to grasp is that those areas at that time, being almost entirely educationally, or in other ways, unwinnowed, did hold some highly intelligent, and potentially intellectual, and imaginative people who had little chance of developing those gifts except by drawing on their very narrow social and educational direct experience.

That aunt of mine who finally made her way to becoming a shopkeeper, serving the fashionable needs of the women in her adopted district, was such a person; her ambition was fuelled by an angry wish to 'get out of this place'. She undoubtedly had intelligence and that was largely native, by nature, not greatly encouraged by her schooling to the age of thirteen. An intellectual spirit or an active imagination were not evident. But, it must be said again, she and those like her who eventually 'got out' were a small minority. Others with those gifts stayed exactly where they were and showed them by developing some demanding craft or hobby, or by intelligence deployed in day-to-day speech and through degrees of understanding nurtured in the course of daily life. In other circumstances many of them might at least have gone on to manage businesses, to do well in technology or, as at least, become middle-range civil servants; or artists or writers or composers. We let almost all of them lie; we just assumed that there was and always would be a huge pool of the largely untrained who were—this was the justification—also the largely untrainable.

Those who thought about education began slowly to recognise this huge omission so that, just before the last war ended, the Butler Act (1944) was hailed as a democratic breakthrough in its definition of and proposals for educational reform. We can see now its crucial limitation: that it reinforced the belief in a three-tiered society. That began to be attacked with the movement for Comprehensive Education but, predictably, that principle is finding the going harder than was usually expected; the entrenched spirit of divided provision is capable of seemingly endless self-renewal.

Intellectual life. There wasn't much intellectual life in the Hunslet's of our big cities; or in the countryside, of course. Again, some who had a spark that might be recognised by devoted teachers were 'brought along' by them and if they were very lucky by other secular saints, or might make their own way. Some of those climbed out, chiefly through the scholarship system at 11 plus. But it would have been a short-sightedly academic eye that assumed that these were the only people in those districts with intellectual potentialities or, eventually, actualities.

Here, one should remember in particular, bring to the front, the Judes-of-the-Back-to-Backs, the 'earnest remnant', to conflate a phrase of Matthew Arnold's with one of Arthur Koestler's. These were budding or would-be (since they had so little opportunity to exercise their gifts) intellectuals. They frequented the public libraries; they had at the least a shelf-full of books, often kept in their bedrooms; a majority of them seemed to be bachelors (the interests occasionally appeared to flag on marriage; though that could happen to some who had not been so socially constrained and had yet for only a while flowered). They tended to be solitary because few around them shared their interests, but they loved to talk when they came upon someone who had a glimmer of intellectual leanings. There were others, naturally, who could not be so easily identified, perhaps married and certainly not solitary, but with enquiring minds. All of this minority were undeveloped intellectuals, undeveloped because they had lacked opportunity and intellectuals because they were interested in thought detached from the everyday, would have liked to *examine* life. They were on the whole treated not unkindly, but were recognised as having unusual tastes, sometimes as 'a bit odd'. Any one of them would have 'given their eye-teeth' to go to a university; at the time very few did, but their interest in hearing about what it was like when someone had reached there was like that of thirsty men asking for a description of a shady and well-watered oasis. Again, the waste.

Imagination. This is the trickiest field of all. To ask again: can you be really imaginative without being to some degree intelligent or, more important, intellectual; and vice-versa? In the sense employed here, the answer is yes. My aunt described just above was said there to be intelligent; but she seemed to lack imagination so that she appeared to be on a single track, unable to see most jokes, or to give a quick flash of a smile at a piece of word play, or—a litmus test—to make or respond to an un-real, surreal, remark, one which can illuminate more than a straightforward drive onwards. It was probably this that made her see life in so cut-and-dried, usually unforgiving because unrelieved and unchanging, terms. By the same arguments, I do not think she was intellectual; she was impatient with ideas, and thought most of them a waste of time, deflecting, mere play, gratuitous. She was intelligent without being intellectual or imaginative. When I became a professor she was filled with pride. This was the fruit of what she did recognise, of hard work and applied 'brains', rather than ideas or imagination.

The other unmarried aunt in that household was all imagination, though it had only limited outlooks, opportunities to show itself. She could express imagination in what Wordsworth recalled as 'little, nameless, unremembered acts / Of kindness and of love', unexpected and out of the way, to which others might respond with 'Eh, you'd no *need* to do that'. So she hadn't, but she was responding to a more imaginative impulse beyond need: Lear's 'Oh, reason not the need'. She responded with and to the demands of the leap in the dark.

Above all, her imagination expressed itself in an almost Coleridgean or Johnsonian way: in words, metaphors, odd images yoked madly or comically together. Probably she did not invent many or even any of those word-plays herself. No doubt some people around her could do that; all jokes don't come downwards, from the educated. She probably had not the verbal confidence to invent her own images. But in picking up and taking over good images she had an unerring ear and took enormous pleasure. Of someone mad with rage she would say: 'Oh! 'er eyes stuck out like chapel 'at-pegs'. On almost any incident of an unusual kind she made use of an image rather than a straight statement. If she saw that a girl was attracted to a young man she wouldn't say: 'she seems to like you' or even 'she fancies you', but 'she'd like to 'ang 'er 'at up with you'. On her, meeting new words and images seemed to have the effect of chewing a mildly hallucinatory drug.

She did not seem to have the intelligence, the intelligent drive, of her older sister, and did not show intellectual interest. Might either of those have been nourished by better education? With her imagi-nation as a take-off point, probably yes.

As her society ordained, she lived well within her own class-world and did not question it. But she loved to hear its odder sides cap-tured in words, to have light thrown on them from oblique angles so that their comic elements were brought into relief. Perhaps if she had been given a better education or wider opportunities, so that she could articulate all she responded to, she might have been—what? A novelist? A stand-up comedian? An essayist or columnist?

There comes to mind now an early and intriguing remark by Raymond Williams. Creativity, he said, could usually find few of the usual recognised outlooks—intellectual, imaginative, artistic—among members of the working class. Their creative energy expressed itself in other ways: in creating institutions, organisations, which ex-pressed their imaginative sense of the needs of their own kind; through mutual help organisations; through the Unions, the Co-ops, the Friendly Societies, Clubs of many kinds and with many purposes, most of whose foundation documents combined charity with shrewd good sense. That idea opens doors. Aunt Lil was not active in organisations, but she lived out a life that embodied her humane spirit.

Behind these three qualities—intellect, intelligence, and imagina-tion—stood the attitudes of society towards them. Many of these attitudes were shared throughout society, were part of what, as has emerged more than once here, can fairly be called components, ele-ments, of a common culture, though within each part there were different emphases. In general, to recapitulate briefly, in the wider culture's public sense of itself intelligence was recognised, intellec-tualism and imagination were slightly suspected, or worse.

The general and long-standing character of attitudes to 'the life of the mind' can be gauged from members of both Conservative and

Labour governments recently. A Tory Cabinet minister dismissed the social sciences as concerned with remote trivialities such as the study of the mating rituals of Asian tribes; and no doubt drew an approving laugh from his audience for that illiteracy. Recent Labour governments pay some service to the idea of 'a whole education', but spend most of their time praising and promoting education for vocation. We are congenitally leery about things which can't be weighed and counted. In 1930s Leeds we obviously had some of that spirit, being hard up. One aunt used to speak admiringly about anyone who was trying hard to arrive at being 'a £5 a week man'; and one uncle talked, it may be remembered, of the indispensability of 'having a good hand' if you wanted to 'get on'.

So one attitude towards anything at all to do with the mind in free action and on display was rejecting, dismissive; such things were not for us. A clever person might be said to 'have the gift of the gab' (mid-17th century), talk 'nineteen to the dozen', or be likely to 'talk the hind leg off a donkey'; that last came down from Cobbett's *Political Register* of 1806. Another had 'swallowed the dictionary' or 'talked double Dutch' or was just 'a clever clogs'. Yet another would be accused of trying to 'blind us with science', or always to 'have his head stuck in a book'; and anyway no one could 'make head or tail' of what he was 'getting at'. One of the most dismissive tags was that someone was 'all mouth and no trousers' (slightly puzzling, that, at first; but very witty, once grasped). To praise a man because there were 'no flies on him' was not to praise his intelligence but his smartness; he was also 'a fly guy' and you could entirely understand (but not trust) him. One of whose talk you could 'make neither head nor tail', who was obviously 'too clever by half', who wouldn't allow you to 'get a word in edgeways' because he was always 'showing off', 'blowing his own trumpet'—such a one was even more energetically put aside. After all, as we saw some time back, 'actions speak louder than words' and 'fine words butter no parsnips'; we don't like 'glib' people. How the adages all roll on and out.

More actively defensive people might intone: 'an ounce of mother wit is worth a pound of learning'. A good instance, that is, of setting things unnecessarily in opposition to each other. Or of the False Law of Undeniable and Inescapable Priorities; as when someone totally expectedly says that we should not spend 'x' pounds on some artistic enterprise because we need all we can spare for cancer research. At such moments that adage, said to be Chinese (we have already noted that the more recherché epigrams usually are so attributed): 'If I had threepence I would hope to spend two on bread and one on a rose', is usually invoked by a 'culture vulture' (not at all a Hunslet phrase). That really is double Dutch or Chinese, to the typical English mentality. That mentality, carried to a simple logical conclusion, would leave us with no roses and a still unmet need for all sorts of inevitably 'more pressing and important things', to which others of their kind would always be added. Roseless, we would continue to quarrel about the priorities between all those growing and 'absolutely necessary' needs.

Defensiveness has its own excusing tags: 'I've never been a great reader', which means 'I've hardly read a book in my life', or 'I really haven't time for reading', though we all make time for what we want to do, such as watching television. I do not undervalue the possible rewards from television. People who have never read a book and are not likely to do so can gain a lot from the best of television: its news, documentaries, investigative programmes, comedy, recreational and nature programmes and much else; so can all of us. The difficulty is that so much on television is designed for distraction and the promotion of the advertisers' offerings, and that proportion is increasing 'exponentially', to employ a fashionable but, here, properly applied and useful word..

Back to books. A Stalybridge housewife answered a knock at the door to find someone trying to persuade her to take out a subscription to a woman's weekly magazine. Her response was at first puzzling: 'No thanks. We've got a book already'. She didn't mean the Bible or *Pilgrim's Progress*; she meant that they already had something with words, a weekly magazine, delivered. That tangentially recalls Snozzle Durante's lines: 'The day I read a book, the day I read a book! Some day—I'm gonna do it again!'. Ironically, there were peculiarly back-handed claims; such as: 'I can read him like a book', from someone who had never been known to 'open a book'. It might be true in the sense they intended, and be an unaware tribute to 'book-learning'. That was joined, as a way of dismissing someone's vaunted attractions, by: 'he's nothing to write home about', from someone never known to 'put pen to paper'.

'It wouldn't suit us all to be clever' is a back-handed admission of inability which is partnered by the occasional frank and rather sad: 'I'm not really up to it—with me it goes in one ear and out of the other'. Of some relatives people might utter a regretful; 'rack his brains as he might, he'll never set the world on fire' or, slightly less kindly, by 'he's a bit slow in the uptake'. A more casual favourite was 'he's not got all his chairs at home'. That was a precursor to a form rarely if at all heard in those days—of today's multiple phrases of the type: 'he's one sandwich short of a picnic'.

But by then we had moved out to people who are markedly not particularly intelligent, intellectual, or imaginative, who are mentally not well-endowed; for whom we had also available another range of phrasings. Some were unkind ('daft'), some euphemistically gentle ('he's not very bright, you know'). Such evasions and many another which are neither unkind nor gentle but simply escapist are brought out more often these days, when it is considered by some incorrect to acknowledge that certain people do need understanding and help, not verbal false comforts and assurances.

Quite on the other hand, there were phrases which indicated respect for 'brains', learning, articulateness. In spite of some traditionally antagonistic attitudes in the streets, a 'scholarship boy' or girl would also meet some rather guarded or puzzled respect. 'He's got his head screwed on all right' / or 'screwed on the right way', 'he's got all his chairs at home', 'the penny soon drops with him'. Even now, when a medium-sized arts and design college up the road here is given the status of a 'University College', the students immediately begin to say that they are: 'up at the Univ'. Status snobbery? Perhaps partly; but the presumed and cherished status has also in some measure to do with the status of universities, of seats of learning.

My grandmother had the remnant of country people's respect for learning, which for them would be invested in the parson and to a lesser degree in the doctor and perhaps even the squire. She never doubted that I should take up the scholarship and not only because that would help me 'to get on'; she was not primarily thinking vocationally. She had some awe about learning and was surprised and underneath deeply gratified when her grandson, just before she died, arrived at that condition by entering the University. Not that she could or, if she had been educated so far, would ever have used language as mildly grand as that. It seems likely that many parents of the vastly increased numbers of university students today still feel something similar. It can be in the voice of the barber down in town when he tells you that his daughter is 'off to the University' (usually in the definite article as though it is one huge, collective place—actually, she went to Leeds) in the coming autumn.

Meanwhile, all around and increasingly, to return to the main theme of this section, multiple voices tell us that 'the life of the mind' matters very little. Those who do try to think can soon be labelled 'intellectual snobs'; claims that one author is better than another in intelligence, intellectuality, and imagination are dismissed routinely as 'elitist'. The only test of quality is head-counting, so one of the long-standing Book Prizes has just announced that it will no longer have an 'informed jury' to decide on the Best Book of the Year, but will take a reader's poll on the choice. Which obviously devalues the meaning of 'best' and replaces it by 'most popular' or 'best-seller'; which, one really wishes one did not have to say, is not the same thing at all.

In such a world there can be no levels of distinction or achievement in literature or the arts or any such endeavours; only the acceptance that the majority must be right. And the PR people will organise that sure-fire conclusion for us. No wonder we hear so much nowadays about the need for 'a level playing-field'. That could be a justice-seeking idiom; or levellingly-populist. This is the world of the mass convoy, committed inexorably to the speed of the slowest; but in which we have rejected the words 'slow', or 'better', or of course 'best' in favour of a dozen sophistries which do not worry or disturb even the slowest, and well suit their Minders, the Ad. and PR. people; we choose the simple counting of numbers.

Hence, by monstrous twists of circumstance, modern society encourages millions of people to continue accepting the low assumption that the arts, intellectual interests and all aspects of the 'examined life', are simply 'not for them'. Once, they were led to think in that constricted way because they were the poor and almost entirely uneducated. Now they are encouraged to continue to think like that, in just as narrow and impoverished a way, because it suits the market to assure them that, in that permanently low-horizoned condition, they belong to the confident, the happy and, in all things even in today's near-literacy and ignorance, the well-endowed, the *right* majority.

After all this talk of intelligence, intellect, and imagination it occurs to me, very belatedly, that another word is needed. Perhaps 'wisdom'. For it would be inexcusable to imply that the three words which have run through this section encompass all the ways of being 'in the truth'. At the risk of sounding sentimental and folksy I have to come back yet again to my grandmother. Of the above three attributes she could have been said to be intelligent, certainly. How

could she possibly have become an intellectual, or even a female
Jude? Until she married she had had no access to books, and marriage brought a line of ten children and still no books or time to read.
Books, other than the occasional popular novel, only entered the
house, through her offspring, when I went to grammar school, and
she was then in her late seventies.

Had she imagination? I think so, but of course it had had to find
ways of expressing itself different from those we usually recognise.
Though she had not had the advantage of any kind of 'book learning', she had acquired as had many others a lived-into power of
judgment. In the light of that, we must have other phrases for such
people and something like self-acquired imaginative wisdom, clumsy
as that is, is the best I can find at present. It is another reflection on
the inadequacies of our culture that we have no easily available word
for this kind of achievement. It includes shrewdness and compassion towards others, and a self-contained, unarticulated reflection
on the terms of life. My grandmother could have in some ways blos-
somed if she had had good educational opportunities; she would
have been able to make more explicit sense of her condition, and
perhaps been moved to change it. That does not necessarily mean
that she would have been happier; she might have been, but that
would have depended also on other more important factors than
sophistication, as it does for all of us. Above all, our state of mind
depends on the nature of the personal relationships we make, wherever we arrive. My grandmother had not necessarily led an unhappy
life just where she was, hard though it had had to be.

It is therefore important to remove from our vision of her and
people like her any trace of patronage by those who have read books,
have learned to express themselves and who feel themselves 'well-
educated'. To remove such traces gives her and people like her their
human rights. If we have ourselves moved, so to speak, outward
and upwards, we can easily forget such a truth which is both simple
and complex, but one which all of us, on behalf of justice to our
predecessors, should try at last to grasp.

*   *   *

Qualified conclusions:

In the last three or four decades, perhaps starting with the *Lady
Chatterley's Lover* trial, large numbers of us have become less easily

shocked by many of the 'rude' words. That is on the whole to the good, though it is not likely to reduce the vulgarity and obscenity of workplaces, streets and bars. The best next move would be to find a suitable word to replace or stand at the side of 'fuck'; we might then discard all those dreary substitutes. 'Make love' will be admirable if it is used only when love is being expressed, is not used loosely or cravenly to describe a loveless fuck.

The languages of vulgarity and especially the languages of sex are changing. At our most sensible many of us do not feel the need for so many euphemisms as we traditionally have had.

The suspicion of the duo, intellect-and-imagination, is little changed except that, moving slightly downwards and wider, the audience that recognises such gifts has increased. Only so far. Below that, the levelling populism rules and tightens its grip all the time. The divisions of social class may be less than they were. The new divisions marked by status, education, and economics are no less strong than the old.

The much wider entry to universities might be expected to increase the proportion of active and trained intelligences right across society. Will it also increase the numbers of liberated intellects and imaginations? That is more doubtful. We know that present governments of all persuasions concentrate on the vocational uses of education at every level; and fewer universities see it as one of their purposes to 'stand for' some things beyond the vocational, to 'bear witness' about the good, the true and the beautiful, the things that are to be weighed not counted.

Most threatening of all, as I have said more than once and will go on saying, is that insistent levelling impulse behind some of the most powerful forces in this society. From them, there is no sign of an increase in respect for 'the life of the mind'; quite the opposite. All those well-established reductive idioms are likely to survive and are being added to; cushioned conformity rules.

To the social and economic deprivations of the underclass in their virtually closed areas is now added the zone of silence above them; they are not worth the wooing; they have been made dumb.

The broadsheet newspapers, on which we used to be able to rely for at least something of an anti-populist voice, seem increasingly unlikely to do other than jump on that band-wagon; the cant image is deliberate, carefully chosen. An example from one such newspaper: In a recent book the author quoted frequently, whilst examining major elements of our common experience, from that great European writer and great European mind, Montaigne. The reviewer took exception to the references; they were 'donnish' and that would never do. Not much sense of the 'intelligent readers' shared, European imaginative inheritance there; rather, an appeal to, an invoking of, the un-intellectual little English mind. Who did that man—who almost certainly was a graduate and perhaps of Oxbridge—think he was talking to in his 'heavyweight' newspaper? Have the readers of the broadsheets truly joined that great majority?

The part played by most intellectuals here is on the whole regrettable. They are too much enclosed within their own groups. They do not need to propose themselves as, in the 19th-century sense, seeking to 'improve the workers'. But insofar as the above pages accurately describe a sorry state of affairs, they should publicly challenge it much more. For the sake of 'the life of the mind'.

8

Live and Let Live

*It is a golden rule not to judge men by their opinions but by what their opinions
make of them.*
                   —*(G. C. Lichtenberg,* Aphorisms—*nearest Hunslet version:*
                                       'I take people as I find them'.)

Tolerance

Racism is the first issue that has to be broached in any talk of
tolerance, beginning, here, with racism among working-class people.
It should not need saying that, so far as it exists at all, racism is likely
to be as common higher up the social scale as lower down. Most
leaders of the British National Party are not 'working-class thugs';
they recruit them; but, again, not only from the working class. 'City
types' too are among their rank-and-file.

Racism still exists, much just below the surface, some explicit,
overt and loutish. The most evident expression is at football matches
where bananas may still occasionally be thrown on the pitch to greet
a black player and the language can be vilely moronic. Those last
few lines were in a first draft of this chapter; they have now been
repeatedly overtaken by events; by racial riots, some very violent,
in Leeds, Bradford, Oldham, Burnley, and elsewhere. In part, they
have been fomented by the British National Party, but that has been
able to draw on deeper wells as some of the results in current Local
Authority elections have shown. One root is the British version of a
Statute of Limitations, the conviction that of almost all things there
are only finite amounts available; the pot is shallow, the well soon
dry. The sense that expansion may breed more expansion is almost
alien to British popular thinking. Hence, characteristic expressions
of British chauvinistic 'limitationism' are: 'They're taking our jobs
from us'; 'there aren't enough jobs/houses/social security funds to
go round'.

Conversely, the long tradition of British hospitality towards refugees, of which we are sometimes reminded in a few newspapers' leading articles, has plainly enriched this society. The arrival of the Huguenots is one outstanding example. Another is the contribution of Jewish refugees from Hitler, and their astonishingly wide and deep enrichments of our intellectual, scientific, and artistic life. That kind of immigration is, as could have been expected, thoroughly documented for the United States. Rather belatedly, a British study of this has appeared (*Hitler's Loss,* by Tom Ambrose), which is very useful, but cannot have the scope of Irving Howe's monumental, *World of Our Fathers*, from the USA a quarter of a century ago.

Many, probably most, people are unaware of that tradition and its rewards. Few schools give serious attention to it in their curricula. There is, deep down in all parts of society, that element of racism, not perhaps virulent in most, but *there*; a sort of elemental fear, which can occasionally, as has happened recently, be fomented into violent action.

Since, as was noted earlier, we almost all like to belong to clubs and similar groups, because that makes us feel warmly part of a enclosed gang, and also because it carries with it the even more comforting sense that there are many others outside, who have not been allowed admission, that spirit feeds racism. We may be surprised by joy to be invited to become a Mason or one of those who possess some royally bestowed honour; but these are ephemeral things. Better to be a non-joiner, on the whole; but very few would be happy to accept that, especially since so very many in Britain join and work—particularly in voluntary bodies—for what they rightly see as the public good. They value 'recognition'.

Many of us fear the in-comer; especially the black one. Our submerged fear increases as the faces become darker. Poles, say, are more or less easily assimilated; Afro-Caribbean less easily. There are other reasons for more or less easy or more or less difficult assimilation, beginning with cultural habits of all kinds, some rebarbative, especially when held by natives of these shores who are peculiarly fast-bound in their own local, and in selective versions of their national, cultures. But initially colour, the degree of darkness, has the more powerful hold.

The last two or three decades have driven some of the worst attitudes underground. But television images can stick. One programme in the seventies included a Leeds policeman who, asked about racism in his force, unhesitatingly delivered violently racist opinions. Nowadays he would be likely to have had some corrective advice. Would it have gone deep or led to no more than cosmetic behaviour?

Until the recent disturbances, and due to the remedial activities of those last few decades, racist attitudes have been somewhat mollified in many of us. We have heard and in parts still hear less about how the arrival of the first coloured family will bring down house-values in the street. There is a coloured trade-union leader. Popular music includes a great many coloured artists among its celebrities, as does the world of fashion. But some people would still not wish to live in an area chosen by a great many coloured immigrants from another continent, as, for example, in Southall with its many Asian families. Those districts are seen as having been 'taken over' and some English house-seekers will strike them off their list of possible places to live. Such simple truths are carefully not uttered by many well-intentioned people; and often resisted if they hear them; yet all too obviously they do not go away, and will not be better understood if we pretend they do not exist.

Perhaps the most deep-seated form of racism, but the most strongly denied by those who hold it and by others who wish they did not, is anti-Semitism. It was there, sometimes explicit in action, sometimes expressed chiefly in language, in thirties' Hunslet. 'Jew-boy', 'sheeny' (a modified form of a word picked up from 19th-century German immigrants, and 'yid' (curiously, that only became truly offensive when pronounced with a very flat vowel) were parts of common speech. Slightly above that level socially, the sneer: 'He's one of *the chosen people*' was common.

Leeds had had, in the last decades of the 19th century, large numbers of Jews escaping from continental pogroms, most of them poor. Eventually and for a time the city was said to have the largest percentage of Jews of any city in Britain. They became one of the mainstays of Leeds' preeminence in manufacturing ready-made clothes. Some, notably Montague Burton, became very rich; and were considerable philanthropists.

Not far below the surface the attitudes of the English were and are, unsurprisingly, complex and contradictory. With us, there was jealousy of the way many Jews worked hard and 'got on'; they were labelled 'money-grabbers'. There was a rather grudging admiration for their strong sense of family and for their recognition of the demands for mutual help. There was some sexual curiosity.

There are still places and institutions, mainly the sorts of club that particularly and unspokenly rejoice in being closed to all but the specially selected and suitable, and which enjoy bars where anti-Semitic remarks are still casually made. Not long ago, the newspapers reported blatant, yobbish anti-Semitism by members of a city Finance Corporation. One wonders what on earth their education, assuming that many have had parents who spent on an expensive education for them, has done for such people; but perhaps that is to expect too much from education in the private sector, even of the expensive type. Many of those schools are too much embedded in little-considered traditional English culture to offer a liberal education.

With many others this racist attitude is like endemic stomach-ache, an uneasiness just below the surface; a sense of wishing to be slightly removed. This often coexists with a degree of admiration for those aspects of Jewish life mentioned above.

It can be touching and heartening to see, in junior school playgrounds and sometimes in senior schools, how pupils of different ethnic groups often play easily together. For some, though, at a certain age and even when they are still in school, something of the deep-rooted racism of home and neighbourhood can leak through and remove or reduce tolerance. Will a common love among many young people of popular music from wherever it comes reduce racist feelings? Into middle-age, when the arteries may harden? That seems a great deal to expect.

As compared with much of the above, some people's attitudes toward those of other ethnic backgrounds, or 'sexual orientation', can be tolerant. It is a long-accustomed tolerance, as may be gathered from the number and age of a great many popular phrases. It is not simply a matter of race but extends to, for example, homosexuals—'a bit odd, them, but who are we, etc...'. In heavy industry, however, hatred of homosexuals can still show itself explicitly and so can low-level racism. There was in the thirties little recognition of, and so of acceptance or rejection of, the idea of lesbianism. One of my aunts lived with a woman friend for most of her adult life. There seemed no suggestions or hints that there might be anything odd about that relationship, or that they were lesbians in the physical sense.

Tolerance towards many, perhaps most, kinds of difference in others can be part of a larger tolerance which still has, in general, more

force than separatism, whether actively angry or just below the surface. On the other hand, some people, one can fairly add, are so
minutely and persistently zenophobic that they will take years before they are at ease with an outsider who has moved in from only
two streets away. These are badly bitten-in people who clutch their
petty 'belonging' round them like a would-be moral chastity belt;
and cannot 'abide' deviations. One learned to understand the kind
of face, or fixed expression, which went with that pattern of attitudes. It is the face of a minority to be found all over Europe, and
probably worldwide

That can coexist with a sort of ingenuous surprise, as when a
neighbour says of newcomers, especially if they are to some degree
coloured: 'They're quite nice, you know. Very civil. And clean'; and
so on, though they may admit that they have had to get used to the
smell of curry. By now, that need not be even slightly racist, especially since large numbers of the population have themselves adopted
curry dishes, and no longer chiefly for eating out.

One of my elderly relatives was a past-mistress of ingenuous surprise. Looking round at a wedding party she noticed a black man
and said without the slightest hesitation: 'Who's the darkie, then?'
'One of my colleagues at the University'. 'Ooh! Well...!' End of
conversation. That was only racist in that she had noticed someone
of a different race and colour and was slightly surprised. It did not
carry overtones of even mild disapproval or drawing back. Her background had, though, taught her to regard black people as strange,
not 'like us'. If my colleague had knelt down after extracting a prayer-
mat from his pocket, or placed his own cooking pot on the lawn, she
would not have expressed any objection, except the usual mild surprise, or at the most, the commonly employed exclamation: 'Well, I
never did...!'

Another said that, in her very poor working-class district, the only
nearby doctor was 'a blackie'. I did catch a touch of disappointment
there and assumed at first that it was because she would have preferred a white doctor. No: it was medical disappointment: 'Every
time I go to see him he just gives me another prescription for Valium;
that's all'. It had been going on for a long time. The contrast with
our Panel doctor of fifty years before was great. My relative knew
she ought to have had better attention, but hadn't had the compe-
tence or energy to seek it. She would have had much the same attitude towards a white doctor who was so lax. Lazy doctors were and

are soon spotted, even if often nothing is done about the fault; medical incompetence is harder to recognise. It requires a good level of literacy to be willing to complain of either.

To sum up here: racism is active and strong in a very small proportion; it is sleeping just below the surface in a slightly larger proportion; it hardly at all exists in what might be called a large minority. These are, of course, impressionistic conclusions, but likely to be as valid as the opinions of those who with no more scientific evidence promptly and categorically assert that racism is now dead; or the reverse.

Adages expressing aspects of tolerance are surprisingly numerous, sufficiently numerous to separate themselves into rough groups, though some easily fit into more than one category.

There are, first, the equable and even-handed: 'Ah well, it takes all sorts to make a world' (that has survived from the mid-17th century), as has 'I believe in live and let live'. 'One man's meat is another man's poison', has come all the way from Lucretius. 'You've always got to give and take', and 'you can't please everyone all the time' seem to be ours; at any rate they are demotic and homely as are most in this area. Fanny Burney observed that: 'it wouldn't do if we all thought alike' was 'a French fashion but fair for all nations'. True; and the English might underline that sentiment with one of their kind of tolerance's key mottoes: 'Life's too short for that kind of thing'.

Then the carefully non-judgmental: 'There's two sides to every question' and 'everyone has faults'. 'What's sauce for the goose is sauce for the gander' is curiously interesting. John Ray in the mid-17th century recorded it as 'a women's proverb'; in other words, to be sexually identified, one might even say feminist before its time; claiming equal rights for women with men; as, perhaps, for as much trouble to be shouldered by the men as by the women. If so, it could have had an extremely wide application.

'There's no accounting for taste' is one of the basic planks in this group along with: 'Take people as you find them' and 'never judge by appearances' (that comes from as early as mid-17th-century Italian) and not surprisingly underlines yet again that the common pool is drawn, above all though by no means wholly, from continental Europe over centuries, with a major line of entry from France after the Norman Conquest, and another strong line from America a few centuries later.

Added to these in our house, indeed uttered more often than many of the above, were the obviously biblical, of which two especially had the weight of rock: 'Do unto others as you would be done by', and 'Judge not that you be not judged'. There was no messing about with those.

Almost at the last is a group chiefly about the need for and value of patience. Some were also putters-off of awkward choices, 'sweepers under the carpet' (I wonder why that is not in early editions of Brewer. Is it so modern? It is not in the most modern Brewer, either). Others were sound acknowledgments of the value of taking your time, cooling off, not rushing into intolerant acts or speech. So: 'Oh, give over', 'Oh, give up—that's water under the bridge now'; and the exasperated: 'Alright, I give in. Anything for a quiet life'; and the wise old 'It's never too late (you're never too old) to mend (learn)', which in various forms has also come all the way from Seneca. It is accompanied by 'least said, soonest mended' and 'leave well alone'—though the 'well' there might be no more than the best compromise possible, as is the qualifying 'well enough'. Particularly pleasant is the sardonic reigning in of 'save your breath to cool your broth/porridge' (from the mid-17th century in various wordings), and the folksy 'hear all, see all, say nowt'. 'People in glass houses shouldn't throw stones' sounds modern but appears in Chaucer's *Troilus and Criseyde* and has since, as have so many others, been so commonly used as to be virtually evenly distributed by class.

Finally, two old nags: the multipurpose 'a nod's as good as a wink to a blind horse', which we inevitably met earlier, and the finger-wagging 'none so blind (16th-century English) as those that cannot see / none so deaf (mid-14th-century French) as those that cannot hear', which sounds foolishly obvious at first until you realise that it is pointing to the habit of *obvious* refusal to use our eyes and ears for those purposes for which they were given. Far from being tautologous, that is good sense based on well-observed experience.

It begins to seem as though there are more well-used adages about the need for tolerance than about intolerance, and more than expressions of racism and religious bigotry. Assuming my thumb has not been on the scale when weighing and counting, that is a pleasant revelation. We shall see whether a broader look at public and private morality reinforces it.

Local Morality

Attitudes towards 'morality' in working-class people in my day divided into two kinds. Perhaps many did not recognise this division, but so it was. It was yet another aspect of the 'Them and Us' duality. Another division might have been between petty (mostly local) and major crime; but naturally major crime was not simply a public, outside, matter; it could become 'private' if that meant that it took place in the local world—a murder in the next street or a really vicious brawl—but those were exceptions.

So 'private' here chiefly means 'local', private to our streets rather than to the larger world and rather than 'personal'. Forms of personal morality have been referred to earlier and will be in the next chapter, especially as they relate to religious belief.

In the enclosed streets, trust operated for much of the time. You did not feel haunted by worry about whether you had locked the front door. There was very little theft by a neighbour from a neighbour. You were 'all in the same boat' so it was something of an unspoken rule that you did not rock it. Occasionally, there were incorrigible youths, usually from a few streets away but soon known, who were going downhill and would steal an unattended hand-cart or rabbits from a hutch; or, noticing you go out for a few moments without locking the door, would risk a neighbour seeing them and nip in on the off-chance of finding a purse on a sideboard. This was truly petty theft. There was no drug-taking to make more serious theft commonplace. By and large, honesty was assumed. Probably Hunslet had its professional thieves known to the police, but they didn't seem to live in our bunch of streets. The coppers on the beat kept to the main road at the bottom; we saw them rarely, usually after an accident or the report of a disturbance.

So we had the usual clutch of reinforcing home truths: 'I hate/can't abide a cheat/a two-faced man', 'crime doesn't pay' (American FBI slogan)—*there's* a vague hope—as is 'cheats never prosper'. Harington in 1618 took that down a peg or two: 'Treason doth never prosper / For if it prosper, none dare call it Treason'. 'An honest man is worth his weight in gold / is the salt of the earth', 'he's right straight'. Another man would 'sell his grandmother if he could make a quid by it'. 'Honesty is the best policy', 'he's as straight as a die / fair and square in everything'. By this point, if not before, it is clear beyond any doubt that many adages have interchangeable versions, but whether they vary according to taste or to history or to fine geographically decided variants or to some other factors, is not yet quite so clear.

'Two wrongs don't make a right', of course; that seems obvious but disposes crisply of the defence of revenge. 'Touch pitch and you'll be defiled'. Above all, 'never tell a fib'. That might at first from its sound be thought Anglo-Saxon. It comes from the Latin 'fabula', a fable. This was a major injunction for us, the George Washington model translated into South Leeds. What with home and Sunday school, we were much affected by the absolute need not to lie. Once, at grammar school during a break in class, I threw a tuppeny 'stink-bomb'. There was a risk of collective punishment, so I decided to 'own up and shame the devil'. That cost me an hour's detention after school every day for the next week. Grandma would have been very shocked if she had known.

Petty crime was not dramatic, more a matter of harassment because often committed by stupid and insensitive people who could cause 'endless' trouble by their greedy little tricks. They caused irritation, considerable irritation rather than downright anger. They ranged from the few small-time local thieves to fiddling shopkeepers and door-to-door salesmen. Those last illustrated the favourite axiom that 'there's tricks in every trade'. They were mildly despised at the least and sometimes worse. They were totally given over to 'lining their own pockets', 'all out for number one', 'all tarred with the same brush'. They 'didn't give a tinker's curse' for the harm done to their victims, were 'any way for a rotten apple', at the least 'a bit thick', 'dozy 'ha'porths' (nice, that}, at the worst heading for jail. They were, as their neighbours reached the pitch of exasperation, 'neither fish, flesh, fowl nor good red herring'.

'Easy come, easy go' (this also occurs in early 15th-century French) was their motto; they could look, especially if they were trying to sell you dodgy goods, 'as if butter wouldn't melt in their mouths', had an air of 'false innocence'. To try to persuade them to improve their ways was like 'throwing pearls before swine' (Matthew 7:6); advice 'ran off them like water off a duck's back' (another of the 'ducks cluster'). Your distress was 'no skin off their nose'. 'They'd cheat you as soon as look at you'. If they tried to justify themselves, you had always to remember never to 'take them at face value'; and to remember also that, though 'many a true word is spoken in jest', many a false word is spoken in apparent honesty.

Sayings around this area are so numerous that you begin to think, in spite of what is said above, that petty theft must have been rife with us, since it appeared to haunt some minds. If you 'give a man like that an inch, he'll take an ell', and he'll be back, because 'a bad penny always turns up again' (18th century), so it's best from the start not to 'touch him with a barge-pole'. That barge-pole rang true; we had canals near and walked on the tow-paths.

Mind you, this sort of behaviour may well be 'bred in the bone'. That adage has a mixed, contradictory history, from the Latin through Malory. It is related to 'blood will out', 'like father, like son' ,and the less bodily human: 'the apple never falls far from the tree'. People like that are 'all tarred with the same brush', though 'it takes one to know one'; and 'I wouldn't trust such people as far as I could throw them' (the only cousin to that so far found is in P. G. Wodehouse's '...as far as I could spit'). Nature defeats nurture, they are implying; there is also implied the existence of an unpleasant, fateful, mark of Cain, an acceptance of the damned inevitability of evil, hanging over that group.

Occasionally, charity intervenes and we say forgivingly that after all, 'he's not as black as he's painted', that if you persist in 'giving a dog a bad name' (the 'dog cluster' again), it will act and go on acting in that way, will live up to its pre-ordained fate. Still, 'it's never too late to mend/learn'. At its mildest you may say that such a one was 'always getting into hot water' (surprisingly, that is drawn from an Anglo-Saxon ritual punishment). The most sentimental of those decides that such a one is 'a loveable rogue, all in all'. In fact, they are probably the worst, all in all.

The 'loveable rogues', small in number or not, were a constant nuisance. Working-class people by definition had little in money or goods. But there was usually someone who would try to relieve them of what they had. It is also arguable that working-class people are at any time more subject to petty but professional crime of many kinds than most other groups. In our day those crooks were not usually neighbours or from the nearby streets; habitual petty crooks tended to work there by day and leave in the evening. The modern 'sink' estates may show different patterns.

Many people are not well-equipped to blow the gaff on the petty crooks in their various disguises; until they have been badly burned, most are inclined to take people at face value—from the well-dressed and well-spoken smoothy-chops selling them dodgy life-insurance to the local spiv offering fake or stolen electrical goods, door to door or in a pub. Many people can be very easily 'led up the garden path' (another of our rustic favourites).

Most—well, perhaps many—get the con-man's measure in the end, but there are always new sheep to fleece. Even today the rampant practice of door-to-door offers of yet another loan at high interest rates to those already in debt can be sure of an endless supply of new victims. We noted earlier that nowadays many of those victims, especially in the more deprived districts, have little or no access to helpful local wisdom, about the money-lending vultures or about many another cheat, hovering around.

Public Morality

Working-class public morality tends to be relativist. The distaste for cheating begins to grow feebler as we enter more public as distinct from local areas. We are not now dealing with friends and neighbours but with bigger, rather faceless and impersonal, bodies. If those firms deal with portable goods—goods which can be smuggled under a jersey or even in underpants—so much the better; and ingenuity can release surprisingly large items under the attentions of a practised hand. Tinned foods from a railway dining-car or exotic refreshments from the first-class cabin of an aeroplane (the British Airways stewardesses' jersey is remarkably capacious, so chest measurements can go up and down) are among the easier stuff for 'nicking', 'knocking off'.

Excuses and euphemisms abound: 'Help yourself', translated, is 'steal'; 'fell off the back of a lorry' (obviously 20th century and probably after the First World War. Not one of my reference books is helpful here), is an all-purpose euphemism for many varieties of theft, and so over-used nowadays that it should be given a rest. You may decide to 'put your hands in the till' or its equivalent, especially if you find that your immediate superior is not above that sort of thing. There may be so much stuff lying around 'looking for a good home', and control of it so lax that a few things taken away 'won't be missed' and anyway 'it serves Them right' for being careless, and 'They can afford it'.

An unusual one, not easy to understand, is 'fair exchange [is] no robbery'; presumably most thieves do not leave a little gift behind. Perhaps it is very cynical, used when a new article is stolen from the place of work and its place taken by a worn-out model smuggled in, thus reducing the likelihood of the theft being detected. A garage mechanic in Leeds told me that a common practice was to book out from stores a brand-new carburetor, say, to replace one more or less worn-out. They would rapidly refurbish the old carburetor so that there was again a little more life in it and then pocket the new one for resale. If the new object was a bit too big for pocketing, they would sometimes toss it out of the window into the nearby River Aire and again, to save time or because they were tired or impatient, refurbish the old one without removing it.

The whole process can begin with, say, the taking of ball-pens home for the family. Many firms 'turn a blind eye' to theft at that very petty level and build the loss into their accounts in some inno-cent-looking way. Working-men's clubs are said to allow their stew-ards up to 10 percent drift in the relation between supplies and re-corded takings, and only to take action above that level. Much the same is said to apply to bar-attendants on ships. Short-changed on a channel ferry by two or three hundred francs, I went back five min-utes later with the change in hand and pointed at it without speak-ing; the cashier equally soundlessly paid up. The ferry operators did not reply to a letter. They probably assumed they could not root out that practice, so don't admit anything and caveat emptor.

In large-scale and pervasive, but still petty, public cheating there are two slightly contrasting rules: bigger firms are more readily robbed than smaller because, as we saw, they seem more inhuman and so to cheat them is not at all like robbing a neighbour. On the other hand, firms that manufacture very large items are obviously harder to rob. Not always, though. Coming off a channel transport carrying soldiers due to be demobbed was a staff sergeant who, once clear of customs, gloated that he had a lorry engine (in parts), stolen from his REME unit, and distributed throughout his kit and those of some 'mates'. He meant to start a haulage firm.

Two final considerations: some—probably many—people, even if they do not practise the art themselves, will not 'let on' (reveal) or 'blow the whistle' (from football), as we say today. We are back with workplace practices. You do not 'shop' (17th century = 'imprison') your mates', especially not to a well-paid management, or even to the police. Second, though both small- and large-scale public cheat-ing are endemic in Britain, we should not assume that matters are more honestly conducted elsewhere. On our first family trip to Italy forty years ago the bank cashier at the border tried to cheat us out of

£30; Italian waiters are notorious for fleecing tourists (and pleading the needs of their large families if found out); the channel ferry mentioned above was French. Europe is as much united in its compulsion towards petty thieving and worse as in its more admirable habits; so are most other parts of the world.

So much for petty crime in the public arena. What of working-class attitudes towards major crime: grievous bodily harm, large-scale robbery, murder? The first and most obvious point to recall is that, so long as they don't touch us nearly, such things are above all a source of immense, continuing, and long-standing curiosity, or *The News of the World* and its near-rivals would hardly have survived into the 21st century. That kind of newspaper, especially if it is one of the 'Sundays', lives much of the time in a state of apparent catatonic shock elsewhere found only in sex-horrified maiden aunts.

It almost goes without saying that there are many phrases handed down from on high about crime and its consequent punishment; that was not quite our angle of approach. Criminals have a vocabulary of their own on all this, full of terms of art. Surprisingly, we seem to have made do with relatively few and some of those wobbly, such as 'crime doesn't pay' and 'thieves never prosper', both wishful thinking. Much more telling in that time and place was 'a tale-bearer is worse than a thief', which underlines the power gossips could wield. There would be talk about someone who was 'doing time' (that goes back to at least the 1830s), or had been 'sent down'; 'in the nick' is street talk. We used 'in jail' or 'in prison' in preference to the preceding evasive three. We occasionally said that one 'might as well be hanged for a sheep as for a lamb'. In the street, that might be used of someone said to have been found stealing ball-pens by the box or copy paper by the ream, knowing that a smaller theft might, if revealed, just as certainly bring dismissal.

We rarely said: 'He murdered her', preferring rather the horrible evasion 'he did her in'. I do not remember anyone reporting that a captured thief had said: 'It's a fair cop, guv'. That was left to conventional crime-novels—or perhaps stage-cockneys.

There could be, though, a strong feeling in favour of retribution and revenge, one almost biblical in its intensity. In any selection of the dozen adages most firmly held to in working-class districts, 'serves him/her/them/you right' would have to be included. It should therefore not surprise that, in the most recent survey on the subject, a majority of the population favoured the return of capital punishment. That we have as a nation ended the practice may be a victory for the argumentative powers of the liberal 'chattering classes' and its seeping-down, and is certainly a sign that Parliament can sometimes legislate more humanely than a referendum might prompt.

Very many epigrams ran and run the other way, condignly. As to retribution, one will hear: 'Give him a dose of his own medicine', 'as you sow, so shall you reap', 'as you make your bed, so shall you lie on it', 'stew in your own juice'. Occasionally, one even hears, in talk about a particularly horrendous crime: 'an eye for an eye'. More mild is: 'You mark my words. His chickens will come home to roost' (as so often, one of this adage's earlier appearances is in Chaucer). More bluntly, 'give him enough rope and he'll hang himself', and 'there'll be a day of reckoning, sure enough' (but always remember 'two wrongs don't make a right').

Revenge is a more individual aim, whether for oneself or on behalf of others. Then you will be intent on 'getting your own back', 'paying off debts' or 'settling old scores'. 'The boot is [now] on the other foot'. This variously used riposte appears yet again: 'what's sauce for the goose is sauce for the gander'. Unexpectedly, laughter appears in several forms: 'he who laughs last laughs longest', 'he laughs best who laughs longest', and 'now he's laughing on the other side of his face/mouth'—the most striking of the group is that last, because the most physically, bodily, conscious. For savage revenge, you will be determined to 'get your knife into' someone, always taking care not in the process to 'cut off your own nose to spite your face' (that can also be uttered as a deterrent to over-hasty revenge). Images about the body, particular limbs and especially the eyes, are inevitably among the most cruel.

It would be a pity and a mistake to end on that retribution/revenge note. On a rough count, there are more sayings in favour of redemption, forgiveness and, in the search for honest living, a more charitable stance, than there are of the revengeful.

We should all aim 'to practice what we preach' (14th century; *Piers Plowman*), should 'draw the line at...(some misdemeanours)', 'set our faces against...(wrongdoing)'—because we know that in the end 'truth will out' (another of the more-hope-than-expectation group), so we must 'tell the truth and shame the devil' (that cluster again), 'speak without fear or favour', refuse to 'run with the hare and hunt with the hounds', and 'keep to the straight and narrow' (from Matthew). We all should recognise that 'good wine needs no bush' (from the bunch of ivy which, long ago, used to hang over vintners' shops), that 'virtue is its own reward' (desperate hope again triumphing over sad expectation there), that 'goodness is more than a pretty face', that there are some people so upright that most of us 'can't hold a candle to them' (being ourselves not fit even to be like the mediaeval assistants who used to hold a candle so that their superiors could see to do their work); yet still 'everyone deserves a fair crack of the whip'.

Such sayings, and there are many, abounded in Hunslet and no doubt in many similar places. How far were they merely repeated by rote? They did seem to be at least guiding lines, even if neglected at times, for many of the people in those predominantly keeping-their-end-up streets. Everyone could 'fall down from time to time', but there was a certain decent coherence about assumptions that bore on the way we should run our daily lives.

And today? Almost all the sayings immediately above, no matter how frequently they may still be used, seem increasingly old-fashioned. And out-of-date? Irrelevant?

*   *   *

So:

Racism is still much with us and in general cuts across class. Sayings in support of it are still alive in all relevant areas. No doubt new ones will be coined though, as is more likely today, in the odious form of 'question and answer' jokes: ' What is the difference between a Paki and...? '

Against those are the aphorisms expressing tolerance. These, too, seem likely to endure, at least with those of us above early middle-age. Among younger people, it is likely that political and social apathy will take the place of, do duty for, an active tolerance; but do it little actual harm. Except that, like a diet of marshmallow, the long term effects could be unfortunate.

Is widespread prosperity reducing local petty crime? One would like to think so. Such a change would not apply to the estates where the underclass live. Nor is the hope justified in more prosperous areas. The links between drug-addiction, theft, and violence are plain enough.

Public crime is as frequent as ever, if not more so; and its many phrases still in use. Some fairly new ones, of this century, are popular, such as: 'it fell off the back of a lorry'. The enormous increase in foreign holidays, and the easy petty crime they make possible, have internationalised theft of all kinds. So far we have, chiefly, warning adages about the wiles of Italian waiters; that kind of thing often does populist service in place of more reasoned judgments.

The belief in retribution and revenge finds its focus in the support for capital punishment. It will be a long time before that majority becomes a minority. Tolerance does not seem to apply there; the sense of public morality stops short of that. One can now find, even in some of the broadsheets, arguments that 'democracy' would be best served if a referendum were held on such matters. The word 'democracy' there is doing duty for a resiling from considered moral judgment, altogether.

It is perhaps worth recognising again here that very many of the idioms cited above are to some extent used across all social classes, but not always in the same way or pattern, nor so often, nor with such emphasis.

9

Many Beliefs

Why, sometimes I've believed as many as six impossible things before
breakfast.
                                    —*Lewis Carroll*, Through the Looking-Glass

From the evidence of their apophthegms, though at the backs of
their minds, working-class people and, it seems, many another draw
on a double or even triple set of beliefs, half-beliefs, notions about
the way the world wags. Elements in each group contradict each
other in the same person; a devout Roman Catholic will go to church
service and take Communion each Sunday and then, back at home,
turn first to the horoscope in that day's newspaper; or will casually
repeat a superstitious adage, without any suspicion that double or
triple thinking might be in play. Different things go in different boxes
of differing weights; in the end the Church's box, at least for Roman
Catholics, may weigh the heaviest of all. But still...

Religion

In the light of the above it is difficult to decide just what the professed faith of many people means at bottom. They continue to invoke Heaven and may pray day-by-day (or, more likely, week-by-
week) almost casually and routinely; they will try to have a seat for
the BBC's *Songs of Praise*—and hope to appear on camera—in the
church or chapel they hardly ever visit; all this without in any way
thinking they may be taking God's name and his commands in vain;
though elsewhere they can say: 'He's the sort of man who will say
anything but his prayers'; and, even more direct and self-involving:
'We must thank Heaven for small mercies'.

Nor does it seem likely that most bother themselves with fundamental religious questions. Many assumed and some still assume an

145

after-life and judgment before God, with God sounding and acting rather like a super-parish-priest, grave and ready to run through the list of your sins in life, but willing 'to make allowances'. Whether God will prove to be a corporeal Being or a sort of Divine Emanation seems to be a question which does not occur.

Much the same seems also to lie behind the even stronger assumption, looked at earlier in more than one context, that we will meet those of our 'loved ones' who have 'gone before' us to 'the other side'. For many the idea of a resurrection seems still to be almost palpable, solid, not a sort of transcendent essence.

Throughout childhood one did not hear such deeper questions or any like them examined or even broached in our house or elsewhere. Yet every other member of our household would have claimed to be a believer. 'It stands to reason, doesn't it, that there must be a God who created this world and us'. Eschatological assumptions without eschatological thinking; the numinous taken simply for granted. One wonders how far recent discoveries in astronomy have or will sooner or later undermine such assumptions. No doubt some Roman Catholic theologians have already demonstrated how the new knowledge may be seamlessly absorbed.

The Armed Forces are or were—they may have changed by now— a hollow but sounding repository, a drum, of these attitudes. It was assumed—it may have been laid down in 'King's (now Queen's) Regs'—that almost every recruit would adhere to some faith; just as it was assumed that only a tiny minority, chiefly Jews, were not upholders of the Monarchy and Christianity; and Jews were let off adherence to the second.

There was an old story told to new recruits—advice, rather, and true advice—that if in doubt you allowed the Sergeant to put down, as his pen hovered over the paper in expectation, one of these: 'C. of E' or 'Roman Catholic' or 'Methodist' or 'Jewish'. He was half-expecting this because, so the story goes, if you did not profess a recognised faith you were, of course, excused Church Parade but were instead assigned to cookhouse duties.

I do not imagine that that was meant to be a kind of punishment, though this was widely believed. Someone had to peel the potatoes for mid-day dinner and, if the majority had marched off to carry out their religious observances, only the agnostics or atheists and the 'just don't know, Sarge's ' were left. Generally, the 'don't knows' were put down as C. of E, not so as to save them from potato-peel-ing but because most Commanding Officers, especially those in charge of wartime Training Camps, who had often been brought out of retirement and tended to love the old Regular Army routines, were likely to belong to the Church of England and wanted a good turn-out each Sunday.

I wonder whether anybody ever replied to that crucial question by adding their own extra conviction: 'Atheist and Republican, Sarge!' The second would have had them up before the Colonel, 'quicksticks'. The combination would have been deeply shocking to people, most of whom had never asked themselves questions about either the grounds of faith or the rightness of being a subject of a crowned head rather than a citizen of your native country.

A friend has added his own touching and brave coda to this story: "When I joined the RAF and was asked to state my religion, I declared myself 'Hebrew-Agnostic'. I was challenged, but insisted that I was a non-believer. It was then pointed out sternly to me that if I was shot down and 'Hebrew' [or 'Jew'] was on my identification tab it would do me no good at all. So I had TWO tabs—one of my preferred choice when at home and the second as 'C. of E'. for flying duty. Couldn't have been many idiots like me."

He wasn't an idiot and the RAF was admirably flexible and civilised, which calls to mind a rather less flexible and intellectually less imaginative military group. I was once asked—just once—to give a lecture on 'British Culture Today' to the national Army College for those Regular (career) officers possibly to be promoted from Major, their present rank. Perhaps that was not a very promising cadre. Almost all the questions came from within the sense of a shared, firm and confident, all-embracing but inadequate cultural understanding, and were all completed with a courteous but resounding and at the same time pugnaciously deferential: 'Sarh!' As in this actual first question: 'Why is the BBC so full of *pinkos*—Sarh!'? Having met three Generals since then, I found the evidence, that the Army can select more articulate and intelligent free-spirits for promotion to the top, comforting.

One would not have expected much metaphysical thinking in the armed services; certainly even less than there was in Civvy Street. There, the Roman Catholics, our story ran, did as their priest told them, whether as to religious practice or in many other matters. Church of England people did not give so much deference to their vicar. Methodists such as we were—rock-bottom Primitive Methodists—

regarded their minister as someone much like themselves though socially higher, of course, but by not all that much (an upper member of the lower middle class, say) emitting little of the 'really posh'.

Of course, many kept—and some still tend to keep—their hands in by going to church or chapel on major religious occasions in the calendar: Christmas, New Year (mainly for the music), and perhaps Easter or even Whitsuntide. Whitsunday was extra special; there were, in many Northern places, 'Whit Walks' round the town (the children in new clothes, usually bought by 'check', credit, of course), with the Church of England and the Catholic walking-snakes carefully routed so as not to meet each other. On Whit Monday our chapel took the Sunday school's steady attenders by train about ten miles out, to a field for tea. Looking back, it is easy to detect a primordial echo in the two spring festivals, with Easter as the early gateway and Whitsuntide as the full welcome to the approaching summer; that sort of primitive expectation did linger at the backs of our minds.

There were and often still are major family moments when we wished to be on the right side by going to chapel: baptisms, marriage (also, perhaps predominantly in many instances, moments for secular display), and deaths. One is forced to conclude that quite without knowing it many, though not the more regular worshippers, had made the old, old wager: best to be on the safe side; an insurance policy taken out on the assumption that God might after all exist. If he proved not to exist when we got up there, then nothing was lost.

That may sound cynical and would be resisted if suggested to a great many people as the real ground of their belief. My wife's spinster aunt, Ann, would have been 'shocked to the core' to hear the suggestion that 'belief' can be seen as a sort of bet. She would have been right to be deeply shocked; she had never and would never have seen it in that manner. She and people like her were not gamblers in any way, least of all in anything concerning their faith; they really did believe; they held their faith 'in the goodness of their hearts' and that influenced their conduct for the better, under God. 'Man proposes, God disposes' (as so many, this comes from early 14th-century French in various forms, but with no substantial change of meaning, all the way up to the present); that was almost their be-all and end-all.

'Influencing conduct'. That brings us to the most evident and perhaps most important aspect of religion as understood by the majority of working people: that it was more than anything else moral, ethical—and moralistic. It conceived of religion as above all a guide to conduct, to good conduct. It is by now clear that, for our family and many like us, 'good conduct' had a distinctly Protestant, indeed puritanical slant. We were congenitally disposed to frown upon those Irish Catholics three streets away who, we were convinced, usually got drunk and probably disorderly at weekends. They didn't seem to have our disapproval of drink, and it was said that some of their priests shared that relaxed attitude. Later, in adolescence, G. K. Chesterton shook some of us slightly by praising the merits of beer. That was surely likely to make them 'no better than they should be', since drink was 'the root of all evil'.

Worse, we could hardly 'abide' the thought of a kind of religion that allowed its adherents to confess their sins, 'say a few "Hail Mary's"' and walk out shriven. At least, that was the simplified way in which we chose to see and believe things Catholic. Our sins were ours and we assumed we would hang on to them until Judgment Day and hope then for fair treatment. Had we known about the belief in the chance of salvation from confession at the very last minute, 'between the stirrup and the ground', we would have joined Aunt Ann in being deeply shocked. Another Catholic tricksy habit, that, we would have thought; trying to play games with God by gabbling a few last admissions and slipping under the gate just before it closed. Our belief was inextricably tied with the duty to try to 'tread the straight and narrow' all the time, and pay the price for 'backsliding' in the end. It was rather joyless; it didn't let us off many hooks during life or at the point of death. It didn't, that is, if we tried to live up to it.

We were in unconscious principle somewhat Lutheran, looking after our own consciences and unwilling to trust them to any intermediary, not to our amiable and rather undemanding Methodist minister and certainly not to a Catholic priest whose religion, we believed, told him to counsel and correct his congregation to such a degree that he took away the responsibility for their own consciences. The more vulgar among us referred to Catholic priests as 'Bog Irish'. We took for granted that they told their flocks which way to vote at General Elections and constantly warned them against birth control; but even by us that practice was not mentioned before children and always spoken in an undertone. We did not like to admit, even to ourselves, that 'French letters' existed and were by now—had been for a long time—a part of working-class married life. Not in grandma's day, though; at that time, the ten-child family was typical.

Not many actually expressed anti-Catholic assumptions; but something like them lay deep down in our nonconformist spirits. As to the day-by-day, that nonconformity, as we saw in the preceding chapter, expressed itself as a manageable, and understandable, set of shared and personal convictions about 'doing right' by other people, being fair, telling the truth, walking a straight path. So the idiom quoted earlier: 'He'll say anything but his prayers', was not merely about someone's secular behaviour; it could also just hint at a valid connection with religious belief. That was what, we believed, our God enjoined us to do. To lead a *decent*—a cardinal word—life. In this, we felt superior to Catholics and, come to think of it, to members of the Church of England. We had not heard that the Church of England was 'the middle-classes at prayer', but most of us assumed it. We held to firm *personal* rules. We were solidly unconforming, truly primitive Primitive Methodists.

It will be noticed that there have been, so far, not many adages about the actual meanings of religion; or about its explicit relevance. That seems a fair reflection of the facts. There are, as we can recall from the last chapter, many sayings about ethics which, we trusted if only half-consciously, were based on our religious convictions. One will do here, to add to the many quoted earlier, especially in the section on morality: 'Do unto others as you would be done by'. That was central, based on more than a sort of humanism, and many people tried to 'live up to it'.

Adages, it is plain, are compact tags, often meant to be helpful indicators. about life and the living of it. The relatively few directly about religion do tend to concern God and His supreme place in our lives. They at least see religion as about much more than ethics. In this they are joined by the Hymns, and those played a part, a remarkably large part it now seems, in our lives; and now in the memories of many of us.

Hymns can be seen as supplements to the epigrams also stored within those memories; not uttered in everyday conversation but always somewhere at the back of our minds; yet, like the epigrams, very easily recovered. It is now many years since I was in a chapel (except for a burial service there, or at crematoria) and I am no longer a believer. But most days I wake with a hymn in my head, and most of them do not go away for the whole day. Why do certain hymns come to mind on any one day; there seems no connection with events that day or the day before, or with dreams; they do not seem to be in any way prompted to the surface by any other event or feeling. They just arrive and go away not by my will but by other hidden impulses. Probably some psychologists with literary imaginations have given the answer. Meanwhile, hymns are as much a part of my working-class background, my childhood heritage, as are all the prosy idioms I have already recalled.

They are almost all about the power and love of God: 'Oh, God, our help in ages past', 'Lead, kindly light amid the encircling gloom', 'Abide with me', 'Rock of ages cleft for me', 'Jesu, lover of my soul, let me to thy bosom fly', 'Love divine, all love excelling'. 'The Church's one foundation / Is Jesus Christ our Lord', 'The King of Love my shepherd is'. Some are sturdy encouragements to ourselves, such as 'He who would valiant be', and many more. They echo the sense of a loving presence to which I no longer have conscious access; but I would be sorry to lose them.

Superstition

Superstitious belief, probably in all classes but particularly in the working-class (for a reason looked at below), can without any sense of contradiction coexist with professed religious belief, and is still amazingly powerful.

That belief has two main branches: first, the belief in something simply identified, though not analysed, as 'Fate', a vague but also pervading element and as often as not malign. 'Luck' is its near companion, like a twin in a folk-tale; 'Luck' is usually assumed to be good luck ('I've had a stroke of luck today'), but 'good luck' can turn into 'bad luck'. 'Chance' sits somewhere between the two, but is nearer 'luck' and is a fancier word with fancier contexts, not much used below the lower middle class. The main point about all three is that they are inherently fortuitous, random, unguided; but still felt even today to play a very large part in our lives.

If your luck is 'in', then your 'number might come up' as in a Lottery (see Job 38:21 for the opposite sense). That is usually 'a good thing'. We did not talk of your number 'being down', but sometimes of it 'coming up' in a destructive as well as a happy sense; as soldiers recognise when they talk of your number 'coming up', of a bullet 'having your [Army] number on it', or insist that 'every bullet has its billet'.

The most powerful numerical hold of all is exhibited by a bad suspicion, that about number 13. Some scholars seek to relate it to a banquet in Valhalla; more connect it with another feast, the Last Supper of Christ and his disciples. How many houses are numbered thirteen? Or city districts (Paris has one)? Or seats on public transport? Or floors in hotels? The hold remains inaccessible to logic; and most presumed sources sound like later guesses. In the ancient world, odd numbers were generally thought lucky.

There are more epigrams about luck being promising than being foreboding, so its adages are very popular: 'Trust to luck', 'better born lucky than rich' (17th century), 'third time lucky', and the doggedly held on to, because it makes an encouraging promise: 'lightning never strikes in the same place twice'. That is not true. The Empire State Building is reported to be struck fifty times a year. A purist might argue that that building is not struck in *exactly* the same place each time, but that would be a niggle. In folklore there are, incidentally, several sovereign defences against a strike. A favourite English one was to sleep on a feather bed.

So they go on. Britain's prosperous mercantile trade from two or three centuries back continued to give us in Hunslet yet another quite unconnected phrase for luck in the future: 'when my ship comes in'. We ritually said: 'See a pin and pick it up / All the day you'll have good luck', but did not usually add, 'See a pin and let it lie, sure to rue it by and by.' Perhaps we filtered out some of the unpromising reversals. Cats, of course, have their own cluster, starting back in ancient Egypt, as fateful creatures. Here, a black cat crossing our path is regarded as lucky; Americans believe the opposite.

'One for sorrow, two for mirth, three for a wedding, four for a birth': It was easy to assume, in our urban/rustic way, that we might be counting there something like primrose petals in a public park. It is much more traditionally countrified and refers to a sighting of magpies. Omens about magpies go far back. By the 18th century in England they were widespread in various forms and rhymes. 'What you lose on the swings you gain on the roundabouts', is a mixed statement. It could be a superstitious epigram about the over-riding power of luck or just a down to earth, hopeful guess at probabilities, as when tossing a coin.

We have already seen that it is a feature of adages that some, on any theme, run confidently in two directions or contain two opposing beliefs: 'A dimple in your chin, your living brought in / A dimple in your cheek your living to seek'. The dimple in the chin was thought to be the impression of God's finger. In America, on the other hand, they say 'Dimple chin, Devil within'. That is one which few, even fleetingly, 'really' believe in, but very many say it when they first look at a baby and note one or the other kind of dimple And few families, even in the assured middle class, would not know how to choose between blue and pink when buying clothes for new babies. They would dress them by traditional sex rules, just in case.

'Bad luck' casts a wide net, as wide as that belief quoted earlier, that 'the young die first' (which is partnered by: 'the good die young'). Except in war, and perhaps nowadays because of motorcycle accidents and similar risky activities that is plainly not true; but it has a strongly fatalistic ring; and a sadness which is hauntingly beautiful. 'Cover her face; mine eyes dazzle / She died young'. No death in old age could earn that wonderful, blindingly regretful, uprising 'dazzle'.

Much more humdrum and depressing are: 'It never rains but it pours'. That is 18th-century English, and usually but not always refers to a succession of unlucky events. Nowadays it more often recalls St. Swithin's day, and the forty days of rain which may follow it. Then there is the oddly inconsequential 'lucky at cards, unlucky in love', though it can be applied to the contrast between success in business and failure in marriage. Even there, it would make slightly more normal sense and expectation if 'lucky', or 'unlucky', appeared in both halves, the other not at all. That would be too ploddingly down-to-earth, too much to be expected, to make a good superstition.

'Walking under a ladder' is still widely regarded as unlucky and not, except by the incorrigibly literal-minded, because something might fall on you from above. On the other hand, only the religiously superstitious would nowadays relate that act to a supposed showing of disrespect towards the Holy Trinity (the ladder, the wall, and the ground making the trio). 'Touch wood' to ensure good luck or ward off ill is not often explained fully by scholars, though some relate it to belief in the prophylactic powers of sacred trees.

Many old superstitions bear on the supposed curative powers of salt. Or, again, the prophylactic. Throwing salt over your shoulder if you have done something that brings ill-luck is, we noted earlier, believed to deflect it; but it must be the left shoulder and thrown with the right hand (as seems no more than natural). That way, you may hit the Devil in the eye. Which recalls the unhappy place of the left in superstitions—left shoulder, left hand, left side of the body and the bed, and a left-handed compliment. It occurs in several languages as connected with bad luck or bad behaviour. Or presumably even, as in our adoption of 'gauche', the aversion can be founded in the dislike of 'cack-handedness'. 'Sinister' is self-explanatory. At school we were drilled out of left-handed writing; it appears that in some schools that discipline survives.

The National Lottery has brought all this into high relief. It crosses most class boundaries, naturally; you may see that in the queues for tickets at Sainsbury's any day. 'Having a little flutter' and 'does nobody any harm' are favourite evasive excuses, but not much used among working-class people. They tend not to see the need for apologies. There, there is always a hope that it might come off because 'you never know your luck'; that would entirely transform a life which, we have had to note more than once, otherwise offers few perspectives. No matter how much you may save you are not going to build up a substantial nest-egg for when you have stopped working; you are unlikely to have an endowment policy and certainly do not have stocks and shares. We therefore need to be charitable if we see plainly unprosperous people spending on the Lottery amounts they cannot 'sensibly' afford.

Someone may feel like pointing out with the best of intentions that £2 a week (not an unusual sum) will take £500 from your money over five years; that may surprise but not dissuade many. It is not really to the point. 'Common sense' says 'no' but endlessly renewed hope wins. A survey has shown that many people in the 'underclass' who, on any 'sober' judgment cannot and 'should' not afford to buy lottery tickets, in fact spend relatively more of their weekly income on the Lottery than people who are better off; that is not difficult to do. Sad; very ill-advised. But to them it can seem like the only possible chance of a way out; even though the odds on winning are several million to one.

This attitude is more charitable than that of those (including some prominent politicians) who like to label critics of the Lottery simply as 'moaning minnies' or 'puritan spoil-sports'. We need better arguments than that.

The second main branch of superstitious belief has to do with the Stars by which, it is widely believed, our Fate may indeed be decided. It moves us over from the merely accidental to the predictable ('it's all in the Stars'). Here enter, massively, all things to do with Horoscopes. Subsidiaries include, to name only a few, reading meanings into the palm of the hand, from packs of cards (such as, occasionally, the Tarot), and from the configuration of tea-leaves. That last was particularly popular with us, being cheap, easily available, and not needing much if anything in the way of training. It all comprises a most flourishing branch of weird and dubious commerce. In a rightly popular current phrase: 'It's all smoke and mirrors'.

The addiction to the Stars and Horoscopes themselves, and directly, offers fewer axiomatic sayings and is inherently less interesting, socially and culturally, than the field of Fate and Luck. Since it pretends to know, it does not have the endlessly uncertain element of Chance. It should be, but is not, easier to shake off than the belief in Fate, precisely because of its claim to predict accurately.

Though it lives by what it asserts are firm forecasts, they can fairly easily be tested for reliability. Not that many of its devoted followers look at or would be greatly shaken by evidence which should destroy its claims. They want to go on believing and the soothsayers help them in this by being masters and mistresses of double-speak, of forecasts capable of being read in more ways than one; they are worthy descendants of Macbeth's two-timing witches.

The whole enterprise is, of course, humbug, whether its practitioners know this or not; perhaps some do believe along with their millions of followers. It seems odd, though, that a graduate of Leeds University is one of today's leading oracles.

But then, millions of graduates and post-graduates and other intelligent people who 'should know better', exchange information with acquaintances as to what is predicted for 'Virgos' or 'Leos' or 'Libras' or whatever. They may laugh as they do so—'only a lark'—but they go on doing it. Almost all newspapers support the interest. For some it would be as unthinkable to drop that as to drop the horse-racing tips; cookery hints would be dropped sooner. Do the editors usually believe what they are printing? That's hard to believe. Perhaps they simply include it cynically, as they do some other regular material, because they know that a majority of their readers will turn to it first. Nowadays, broadcasters have jumped on that wagon; 'after all, if 'x' million people want it, who are we...'? It is yet another extension of the definition of 'Public Service Broadcasting'; if broadcasters still feel a need to use that justification.

It is all like watching the bulk of a society peering for signs, engrossed, into an ancient black hole whilst flying at 39,000 feet in a marvel of modern, entirely secular and physically explainable technology; and recognising no disparity. It is not so much a throw-back as a continuing adherence to truly elemental superstitions, pre-Christian beliefs, by people, many of whom would claim also to be Christians.

Together with Fate and Luck, the Stars and Horoscopes continuously interest—almost preoccupy—if not most of us, then more than does reflection about whatever religious belief we may profess. So here is yet another evidence of our ability to keep two contradictory convictions in suspension at the same time. It is curious that we also say, dismissively: 'Oh, that's no more than an Old Wives' Tale', as though we recognise it for the delusion it is, though we daily continue to swallow dozens of such tales (George Peele had a satiric play with that title in Shakespeare's day, 1595). What can be the right phrase for this condition of believing whilst not believing? Dual or treble belief? Shared and conflated belief? Multiple belief? None of those fits.

Time

We need to come back here at slightly greater length to something briefly looked at before (in chapter 6, then chiefly in the context of Work): Time, the sense of Time, brooding and hovering over everything, is psychologically related to that of Fate, and has a similar hold. All too clearly, Time, with Memory, is endlessly interesting because it is an inescapable element in experience. Ever-present, it lurks, benignly or threateningly, over all our doings. We still use old-fashioned images rather than figures to indicate its passing: 'Oh, that was donkey's years ago' and 'that'll happen when the cows come home'—though that certainly doesn't mean 'twice daily'; more likely, 'never'.

It does not surprise that epigrams on Time are sometimes happy, sometimes unexpectant and cautioning, sometimes melancholy. Let's walk awhile 'down memory lane' (that must be pleasant), let's talk of this or that 'for old time's sake' (though that may, one supposes, involve telling the equivalent of sad stories of the death of kings), 'tomorrow is another day'.

Aphorisms on Time prove to divide easily into two main groups: the practical, the everyday, the hortatory; and the more numinous and brooding. The first include: 'Time is money', 'no time like the present', 'one step at a time', 'taking time by the forelock' and 'time flies'.

On the other hand, there are the at the least slightly ominous and foreboding sayings: 'Time and tide wait for no man', 'time will tell', 'there's a time and a place for everything' (a favourite off-putting injunction with us), 'in the nick of time', 'time immemorial', 'third time pays for all' (might be cheerful), 'time out of mind' (a classic of the kind, because it recognises by unconscious refusal the usual pre-occupation), 'Time, like an ever rolling stream / Bears all its sons away…', 'never is a long time' (that, too, could be hopeful), and a rather lonely runner-up, 'time is a great healer'.

Fate, Luck, Chance, the Stars, Horoscopes, Cards, tea-leaves, Time—and religious belief. With all their often-conflicting epigrams to guide us, they make up a strangely rich brew; but one whose components we rarely examine or question; which doesn't seem to upset our mental stomachs, and from which we almost all drink most days.

* * *

Looking back:

Though the decline in religious belief shows no sign of ending, some of the 'truths' once founded in religion—such as in the existence of an afterlife and meetings with one's 'loved ones' there—still seem strong.

As to the hold of the various kinds of superstition—Fate, Luck, and the rest—there is also no sign of weakening. We continue to avoid ladders, have views on fallen pins and the uses of salt, shun the number 13, and have mixed but often sombre views on cats.

All this undoubtedly meets, well—feeds—a deep-seated and un-changing need in most of us, a need now constantly fed by popular newspapers and magazines. That is presumably why there is no sign of a moderation of that need, especially as concerns Luck (or Chance), the Stars, and Time.

The success of the National Lottery is the latest and supreme ex-ample of the attraction of Luck, apparently across all social classes except perhaps the highest. Perhaps—probably—they, too, are in-volved, as much as some of them are with the taste for hamburgers and milk-shakes. The Stars—'it's in the stars'—also retain their hold.

They are believed in, as predictors, by many; half-believed in by many more. That puzzling condition of 'half-belief ' surfaces again. Here, newly minted idioms seem not needed.

Above all, Time haunts us, a presence—a threat, a promise, and with several characteristics in between—which we cannot shake off, so that it comes to seem not simply a physical element, but a positive, a determining force in our lives. We have plenty of aphorisms around that, too, and probably do not feel the need for more, whatever modern astronomy may suggest.

10

A Gathering: And a Glance at Today

*The future is made of the same stuff as the
present.*
　　—*Simone Weil*, 'On Science, Necessity and
the Love of God'

*Time present and time past
Are both perhaps present in time future,
And time future contained in time past.*
　　—*T. S. Eliot*, Four Quartets, 'Burnt Norton'

Together and Apart

Among the more evident findings of this moderately long haul
are: from what a wide range in space and time come many adages
still in frequent use, and how few seem to die (though to prove that
would need another and more difficult enquiry). To predict which, if
any, of the idioms created in recent decades, most of which probably started as 'sound-bites', will survive would also be to pose a
different kind of question.

Another evident finding seems to be that, though there are some
idioms which were almost confined to that group of working-class
people observed at the start here, most of those commonly used are
drawn from the national pool, part of a common culture one might
say. Differences between class outlooks indicated by their linguistic
habits are therefore to be discovered from identifying not only the
body of idioms used, but from defining which are used most often
and with most emphasis by each class. Not a surprising result but
useful, since it suggests both shared experience and some particular
and different reactions to it.

That adages, apophthegms, epigrams and the like are over-used
is a tribute both to their handiness—they save time and thought—
and their attraction; they almost all use images and we almost all

159

love images. They are often pictorial, colourful, striking in a way we had not ourselves thought of. They yoke what seem like disparate things together in ways we had also not thought of, until it was done for us. They can be neat, alliterative, attractively counterbalanced. Sometimes they commit vulgarities for us, and get away with them on our behalf.

They can be employed in all sorts of contradictory ways, they do sometimes contradict each other or even themselves; we either do not notice or do not mind anyway. We 'pick and mix' between, like magpies attracted to bright fabrics, even though some of the objects' brightnesses are, if we look closely at them, meretricious. We do not look closely; even bogus brightness, especially when witty or apt, can win.

If there were an annual *Trial of the Pyx* for epigrams as there is for the national currency, many would have to be thrown into the linguistic pot each time for melting down. They no longer have enough weight; they have become thin from excessive use, some over a quite short period. Their butterfly—or midge's—flight causes them to be soon consigned to linguistic outer space, verbal rubbish.

Some popular recent ones never had much weight to begin with so that one is slightly surprised that they were even taken up. What ungifted person invented: 'I'll give you a bell' which has largely succeeded: 'I'll phone you' or even: 'I'll give you a ring'; what leads people to adopt such an uninspired substitute? Simply the desire for change of any kind? Because it can sound knowingly salesmanlike? Even the much abused: 'dead on the water' sounds lively by comparison. 'dragged kicking and screaming into the 21st century' is as boring as that 'bell'.

Some sayings are born clichés, some become clichés by overuse; the 'bell' and that 'dragged kicking...' belong to both groups. A few start quite well but degenerate into clichés before they are allowed altogether to fade away. But in these pages 'cliché' has almost always meant an idiom which was probably never inspired but lingered on chiefly out of speech laziness. Most of the inspired ones cannot fairly be said to have degenerated into clichés, though certainly they are likely to have been overused, just because of their attractions. This is a narrower definition than that of Eric Partridge.

Perhaps some linger because, although they may be over-used and so avoided by careful writers, they retain for many of us an almost fresh force; they may have a catching, universal-seeming simplicity so that we would be sorry to see them go. Such are: 'Birds of a feather stick together', 'the boot is on the other foot now', 'that puts the cart before the horse', 'he's the apple of her eye', 'six of one and half-a-dozen of the other', 'not for love or money', 'I'll take pot-luck', and dozens of others. What they say is elemental, basic to our common experience. It seems a pity even to call them clichés in comparison with others which certainly deserve that title. It will not surprise any reader of the preceding chapters that of those seven, chosen at random, three or four draw on experiences from our rural past.

Some new images quickly take over from the older, or live side by side with them, in the mouths of different ages and types of speaker. 'He's been as sick as a dog' is succeeded by or runs parallel with: 'he's as sick as a parrot'. That is particularly strange. Not the dog image; dogs have shared our lives for centuries, so that we have almost all seen a dog retching after eating something rotten out of doors. But why has 'parrot' become so popular nowadays? They, too, have been around here for some centuries and are prone to several nasty diseases; perhaps that explains the image. Is the current vogue a response to the hugely popular parrot sketch in the *Monty Python* show on television?

Aphorisms and Social Change

We began with aphorisms inspired by the condition of poverty before the last war and for centuries before that, and, for those who endure it today, still likely to be relevant. The question was: did they reflect poverty's main characteristics, centred on the strain of 'putting up with things', whether stoically or cheerfully? Many sayings underlined the overwhelming presence of that response to a continuing struggle. 'Making ends meet' was a related cardinal activity. Given the number, nature, strength and repeated invoking of these sayings, the hunch that the condition of being poor had to be given first place in this book has been borne out. It seems very unlikely that any other class has had so powerful and tight a clutch of adages-to-live-by.

And today? Though many people are much better off, many of their underlying, inherited and lived-into attitudes can still fairly be called 'working-class' The argument popular thirty years ago: that the working-class were being *embourgeoisified* was neither true nor helpful. We do not become middle class by acquiring certain habits that formerly belonged to the lower-middle-to-middle-class world. You do not, unless you are an exception, go to middle-class pubs, or golf-clubs, or even Garden Centres, or to the Army and Navy Stores or Marks and Spencer, with or without a handful of Store Cards. Nor, to enter a different stratum, do you read many books or take a journal of opinion. To be working class, or middle class for that matter, or probably upper class—all these, as was argued earlier, are above all states of mind, deep-seated and not easily changed. Yet many working-class grandparents' and parents' favoured idioms are sure to fall into disuse as prosperity and its inevitable concomitants take over, assuming we do not run into an economic depression.

For the purposes of these essays, it was necessary to juggle chiefly with the old social categories, some of which are likely to become increasingly inapplicable not merely to prosperity but to newer social divisions. The long flirtation with the concept of 'classlessness' should be left with those in the middle classes who do try to recognise change but wish to do so without making unpleasant discoveries in the process. For them, the saying: 'we are all classless nowadays' is a life-belt, made of pressed paper. We need instead to set about, very carefully, identifying and naming the new groupings; but not here, except tangentially; that needs another and much fuller enquiry. It has already begun, but not much more than that.

The divisive and increasing prosperity is one fundamental starting-point. But the division between that large majority (though that needs to be sub-divided) and the minority of others left behind is increasing. That, too, is commonly agreed. Successive governments have tried to grapple with the situation, though so far not very successfully. Many are confused by a misunderstanding of the meaning and implications of the concept of 'meritocracy', and so of its limits as a desirable social principle. Meanwhile, as was noted very early, it is regarded as callous to use the one phrase that fairly labels the losing group: 'the underclass'. That has, spoken aloud, the too-shocking power of a modern version of the child's cry: 'But the king has no clothes'—revised into 'But these people have no money. They are an underclass'.

It is worth again underlining that most members of the underclass, most 'sink' estates and areas, have not, in the nature of things, a strong sense of community, of neighbourliness. If virtually all of those in those places are in desperate need of more help, who will provide the supporting neighbourly attention? Hunslet in the thirties would have sunk under today's weight of deprivation; 40 percent were on Social Security by a decade ago. The pattern of their most-used epigrams is likely to have been drained of those about sticking together, mutual help and keeping your end up, in favour of those more despairing phrases about there not being much to hope for. Today, to a 'poverty of expectation', which was limiting enough, has been added a drained 'poverty of spirit'.

If poverty had not been put first here, then that place would have had to be given to the sense of family and the language for express-ing it; the hold of that is inextricably bound with the knowledge of being poor. But it is not unique to a class as the sense of continuous and permanent poverty can be, nor is it confined to Britain. In virtu-ally all the families one comes across in almost all countries, whether in actual experience or through books, the sense of family bonds is one of the strongest of emotions.

So, no cross-national comparisons have been implied here; or cross-class contrasts within the same country; except in varieties of habit, gesture and expression for drawing upon similar emotional roots. It is sufficient to stress again that the sense of the importance of family was, and probably still is, extremely powerful among the English working class. It was and is evident in other classes also, each with variations, local characteristics. In the working class it found its most obvious expression in the extended, usually the three-tiered, family. It was also encouraged by 19th- and early-20th-century huddled, urban working-class housing; need and intimacy came together; the one bred the other.

The archetypal pattern was: mother and father and the younger children in the central household, married sons and daughters two or three streets away; and grandparents (unless they or the survivor had already gone into a son's or daughter's home; or to an Old People's Home) were also very near. Landlords were normally ex-pected to respect this grouping when houses to rent came up. Chil-dren still at home, unless there was 'bad blood', ran between the points of the triangle, especially to 'Gran' ('Nan' in more Southern parts); or expected to see them regularly at their own home. It was all a very complex interplay of movements and mutual assistance.

It has weakened; it had to be weakened. High-rise flats were soon after the war major destructive elements. You don't easily nip down sixteen stories; you cannot easily 'just drop in for a few words'. Floors apart, huge blocks apart, discouraged much of the old intimacy. You could feel hugger-mugger with many you hardly knew, without feeling 'close to your own'. New housing areas did more to break the three-tier network unless, and it did happen, a local housing authority mixed generations on its new estates and filled them sympathetically. The emergence among working-class people of old or oldish motor cars produced the mobility which allowed the ways of the extended family still to be at least partly in action, even when distances between each generation were much greater. The extinction of the 'workhouses' and the later rise of Old People's Homes could reduce one long-standing nightmare, but replace it by a more complicated set of questions. It is not as simple as it often used to be (unless you belonged to those who were entirely disinclined) to take into your home your widowed mother/grandmother, even if you feel in yourself easy about doing so. With both husband and wife working and the house empty most of the day; there is no one to give much attention to an eighty-year-old. And if the parents wish to go on a foreign holiday who will look after the aged parent? If you are lucky, one of the other siblings will. The old tradition can survive more than one might expect. Some, perhaps most, people have a sense of family obligation and find a solution; but the strain of upholding the old model is inevitably greater than it used to be.

As more people become mobile in their work and are required to move at least once and probably more often, so the attitude described in an earlier chapter ('We're Newark people. That's where we belong') will become less and less easy to hold to. This more open and fluid process will plainly be pushed on by the communications revolution and its resultant freeing from fixed industrial and commercial locations.

It may be that the huge increase in numbers receiving higher education, more and more drawn from parts of the population which hitherto put few through to that level (though the latest figures show that there is still room for expansion there), it may be that that incursion will be another spur to yet more movement among and between groups which had before thought as themselves bound to a native town, occupation, habits. That may become one of those elements of attitude-filtration and inter-action signalled earlier. It, too, would then contribute to the loosening of traditional working-class family ties. But, as always, slowly.

As all these changes take place so the large network of sustaining phrases must change. With profit and loss. Those that drew on a dog-in-the-manger resistance to movement physical or mental will gradually fall away; good riddance, on the whole; we are 'well shot of them'. So will those which express a network of neighbourliness; phrases expressing the life of what social scientists call nuclear and atomised families will succeed.

As to changing habits in eating much has been said earlier, most of it cheerless. The broadsheet newspapers use considerable space in talking about the improvements in British cuisine, the French chefs who have happily settled here, the Michelin stars now awarded. Let us take that at face value. It only affects a smallish section of the population, say about 15 to 20 percent; though it is probably growing steadily. They are the people who turn to the restaurant sections of their newspapers quite early, who are prosperous enough to eat out regularly, and who often have expense accounts and the posher kind of credit cards. They do not all live in London, and assume that 'You can't trust aubergines north of Watford', as one food writer warned; but that was about twenty years ago. They belong to and should be put in their separate compartment when eating habits are being discussed. But that is still not enough. They belong also to that wider group: of that 20 or so percent who now form Group A, the top-dogs, in this more and more stratified (as distinct from class-defined), more and more meritocratic, society. How they eat is only one of many defining elements in their way of life and not the most important; a sort of cosmetic sign, rather.

Until and if the often lamentable changes in eating habits below that expensive level change, the *haute cuisine* writers, especially in the superior Sunday papers and the more intellectual weekly journals, will continue giving the rest of us mistaken ideas about what really is happening to English feeding, for and by the great majority of the population.

The old phrases indicated a sense of the need to feed your family properly. Among the very poor that did not often succeed as the revelations about malnutrition in the two world wars showed. Most families in work knew the value of a good table and how to arrive at it economically. It is easy and in some respects tempting, in the matter of food and cooking among working-class people, to enter into a lament for times past; when Mum with a few vegetables and scraps of meat could turn out a nourishing stew for six. Still, she had been taught to aim at that; the right tradition had been passed on to her.

Yet a recent survey, mentioned earlier, showed that many wives now have little idea of how to cater for a family in that way. The tradition has more or less gone. There are some obvious causes: if a majority of wives and mothers are out at work all day they have neither the time nor the inclination, being tired, to set about cooking a 'square' meal. It is easier to bring something in and put it in the microwave. What may be brought in will be drawn from two main sources: the prepared meals which the supermarkets produce in ever-increasing variety, and the proliferating outlets of the fast food industry. The diet-sheets produced by hospitals and other public services may include almost all such foods in their 'Not Recommended' columns, as having too many additives, especially sugar and fats. But most who buy those foods regularly do not read official diet-sheets. They might do better to choose more carefully between the suppliers of prepared dishes; but Marks and Spencers, for instance, are markedly dearer than the rest. Members of Group A in a hurry go there, or to Waitrose; once again, better off and more sophisticated people win. Here as so often, the gap seems always to widen, most powerfully pushed on by differences in available money and in education. It is also and probably just as much increased by the vastly greater pressure from the fast food markets to take the available cash from those millions; that can be an even more profitable activity than taking their money from the smaller number who graze higher up the hog. The gap may be widening and is certainly deepening. And the fast foods firms' products continue to meet that major, powerful, working-class demand: they have to be, above all, 'very tasty'. Very tasty, indeed.

As to 'drink', 'booze', alcohol, the picture is somewhat simpler. Manufacturers continue to try to capture niche-markets, as they did just after the last war, with Babycham directed especially at working-class girls, for whom it seemed to have something of the aura of 'bubbly', and anyway was safer than stronger drinks if you were being taken out by, or being offered a drink out of the blue by, a young man who was chatting you up, and about whose intentions you were not yet sure.

How long ago that seems, like black and white cinema films, in this era when new pseudo-pop but quite strongly alcoholic drinks with catchingly comical names, directed at teenagers, appear in a rapid succession. This is a rotten trade. Even worse is the growth in spiking young women's drinks with disabling drugs which make them easy victims for molesters. That is, of course, a criminal act. Selling the new pseudo-pop but alcoholic drinks for teenagers is legitimate, but, if the word is still in our shared vocabulary, wicked.

A major change here has been the increasing consumption of wine; starting in the middle classes and working its way down. Only the other day a self-employed craftsman told me that he and his wife liked occasionally to go out for a meal nowadays, 'with a bottle of wine'. They had, it seemed, acquired that habit as agreeable, civilised, something to which they had only recently felt able to aspire, the children now being old enough to be left safely or with a baby-sitter. He added that they had been to an Indian restaurant (which has its own defined place in these changes) in their small town. He was piqued because they had been charged £22.50 for a bottle of wine— 'Which I could easily have got for about £3 in Tesco's. Next time, I'll remember to look at the prices first'. Changed habits call for some complicated shifts in practice.

Though wine-drinking is increasing, beer-drinking still crowds many pubs even on weekdays. In almost all areas beer is inexcusably expensive; and meddled with. A good German beer is in another league for quality. But, apart from CAMRA, the Campaign for Real Ale, which is a minority activity, no one seems to notice or mind; and the swollen beer bellies proliferate. Many university students, unless they are particularly hard-up, would think themselves deprived if they did not regularly pass their Saturday nights, at least, in the crowded Union bar or an equally crowded local pub. We have entered the 21st century with a huge swathe of the population virtually afloat at weekends on industrialised beer. One must hope that many younger people go not chiefly for the beer but for the continuous talk with their friends, perhaps in the hope of picking up girls, or boys; and because to do all these things is to pass through one of the main, more desirable, rites of passage. Orwell would have had to learn a new language if he were to feel at home in the crowded bars of today.

For many, more 'disposable' money, and more and different things to spend it on: that is one major new element. Since most no longer live in the cramped back-to-back streets, they do not experience neighbourly poverty; the massed epigrammatic speech inspired by that in even their fairly near forebears is not theirs. It would be foolish, by an almost automatic response, to regret those changes. It would be good to think that the knowledge of that language, and the life it was drawn from, were remembered by at least some, as part of their family history, that record of deprivation and also of endurance.

As to health, the contrast between pre- and post-war shows great differences; much gain, some loss. The old Panel system could be good if you had a good doctor nearby; we had, and owed a great deal to his devotion. Other doctors could be so-so; our kind of people, being indelibly marked as the poor, were often more or less treated as such.

Those gains were made by, above all, the creation of the National Health Service.The debt to Attlee's government there (and in particular to Aneurin Bevan), and in other areas reformed by the first post-war government, is also now recognised by too few people. Indeed, some are now in the business of minimising those advances. It was, in fact, a heroic period.

And today? In spite of all the often overheated and prejudiced criticisms of the last few years, the National Health Service is in many respects a model for a democracy; to someone who had known health provision only in the thirties it should have come as an admirable revelation. Teeth now are not ugly gnashers, spectacles do not so often resemble bottle-glass, hearing-aids are not so protuberant and inadequate; those are some of the more evident advances, if not against life-threatening conditions. As to the life-threatening, even those who criticise the NHS and pay for private medicine know that, if a serious emergency arrives, you are usually best advised to go straightaway to your nearest National Health hospital.

The most glaring and rarely admitted anomaly in today's service is that it is divided, two-tier; and that division is decided by the purse. This is the most unjust of its features and one which most governments, including the most recent Labour administrations, hardly dare touch; the red-hot poker of the Health Service. If you opt out of the state system and pay for all your health care you do not, again, necessarily receive better treatment. You may, on occasions, be sent to a pre-eminent consultant, though that will usually cost more. You may be treated, as a person, no better than you would be in the state system; most NHS clinics and hospitals do not treat you as a second-class citizen today (though I know one which, in this, still has the manners of many a thirties local infirmary). In private hospitals you are likely to be treated rather differently, not more humanely but with some added deference, rather as if you had booked Club class;

and coffee is always available. Of course you are given these little upper-crust creature-comforts; the P.R. officers of the private sector would be falling in their duties if they did not suggest that these and other touches are markers of desirable dividing lines between pay-ers and non-payers.

No: the overwhelmingly most important consideration which sways most people who opt for private treatment is not that it en-sures better treatment, but that it cuts corners; it is essentially a queue-cutting device. Those who say that private treatment helps the NHS by reducing queues are defensively blinded and illogical; you do not help a public service meant for all by turning your attention first to those who can pay; that *lengthens* the waiting-lists for the others who cannot pay, some of whom may be in more urgent need.

To give examples is easy, and only those incorrigibly committed to defending private care will refuse to accept them. A friend's wife needed a cataract operation; her local NHS Hospital in London had a year's waiting-list for that. She asked what was the waiting-time for private treatment. The consultant handed her a card: 'Phone my secretary. I can fit you in during the next two weeks'. The other case concerned a man in need of early major heart surgery; his local NHS hospital had a waiting-list of some months. His wife was especially, and naturally, appallingly worried. They had savings and asked about private treatment. A surgeon saw them on the next Saturday morn-ing, confirmed that the matter was urgent and did the operation in the following week. Incidentally, the surgeon was heard, outside the consulting room before he made his first examination, upbraiding his attendant juniors for having asked that particular patient to un-dress *before* he was to be seen. 'Hadn't you realised that he is a *private* patient'? The better cultural and social education of many consultants and specialists is long overdue and obviously must start in the medical schools. Some are already imaginatively liberated. Others, incidentally, add racism to their other short-sightednesses.

Did another patient die because that lucky man had used his purse to secure a place? One could go on. This is the scandal—the word is not excessive—at the heart of the Health Service today.

A curious by-way. Of three Asians (two consultants, one a G.P.), whom I have seen within the NHS, two treated me in a most superior manner. One, when I asked him to explain further an item of advice he was giving, asked: 'Do you understand plain English?' Puzzling. An English specialist would hardly have asked such a question, and so rudely. I wondered then whether, since Asian consultants are likely to have been drawn from superior castes, some simply assume that any English person who uses the National Health Service must be of a lower caste and to be addressed as such.

To return briefly and finally to neighbourliness. Those of us who stress its power in earlier working-class areas, and also stress its links with the need to help one another because to pay for help is not possible, are right up to a point. We are mistaken if we imply that, say, middle-class people do not practise neighbourliness; they do in many kinds of ways. They also have something rather different, a ramified practice in freely chosen, not place-bound or need-bound friendliness. That working-class people did not have this is, clearly, not a sign of their unfriendliness but a result of circumstances: re-stricted mobility, different situations at work from those in other classes, little available money; and so, overall, different long-stand-ing customs governing social behaviour. The new working-class are learning some things, slowly but steadily: sleep-overs, text-messag-ing, meals in Indian restaurants—with wine.

The formerly mixed but largely unitary working-class neighbourhoods have mostly shrunk, most of those who could get out have done so; many of the rest belong to the underclass. A woman who found herself trapped in one because her husband could not keep any job for long told me that her early-teenage son walked in one day and revealed that he and others had violently beaten an-other, smaller, boy. When she remonstrated with him his prompt answer was: 'Well, that's what it's all about, I'nt it? Yer've got to keep yer end up'. A dead-pan motto for a dead-end district.

Death (to continue running through themes one by one, as they appear in the earlier chapters, but now looking in particular for the effect of changes): favourite aphorisms on death show few alter-ations. Why should they—except for newer routine phrases brought out by, in particular, the attitude to cremation?

The nature of work, employment, is undergoing some of the great-est of all recent changes. Thatcher's depredations on the unions (par-tially justified) made them even less prepared than they might have been to meet the much bigger challenge which was coming up quickly; globalisation. Globalisation requires new approaches and new languages from both workers and their unions, and those are not easily acquired by either. It is sad to see some union leaders (though, in general not those at the top of the Trades Union Con-

gress) and some politicians stuck—if their language is a true indication—in the postures of thirty or more years ago. That produces, in
conventional educated idiomatic phrasing, a dialogue of the deaf.
An all too typical sight in the new century is that of a local union
boss upbraiding 'the management' in all the old language of moral
postures, when the top management are thousands of miles away
and have based their decision to close a particular plant entirely on
global decisions about profitability.

A more encouraging change is the movement of women, especially of wives and partners, into full and part-time work. The need
was there, abundantly, but resisted in many places. Yet employers
needed more employees and women wanted the money; feminism
put justification behind the two. So women flooded into part- and
full-time work, according to mutual needs. It is still, rightly and powerfully, argued that the glass-ceiling is cracked not shattered. But we
should acknowledge an important change when we see it at least
emerging. What we now see, in some great concerns— financial,
commercial, industrial; and especially in communications—are more
women at or near the top to an extent that would not have been
expected a few decades ago.

What are being referred to here, in a catch-all phrase, as 'manners' have been undergoing some of the most subtle changes of all
across society as a whole. They are rooted in the sense of class. That
is still pervasive, its denial a continuing self-deceit. The definition of
some of its new groupings could do with much more fine-tuning,
but the sense of separation remains, is being continued and promoted, at least with those who want a drawbridge, and that pulled
up; and who still work at keeping it in that position

It was argued earlier that the emotional energy formerly expended
in maintaining old-style class divisions has been transferred to maintaining new status divisions. The emergence of these new social divisions and their expressions are especially firmly shown in educational and health provision; these are two major instances of the
deep-seated English sense of separation and of its capacity to reinvent itself as society changes. Less evident but in the end more
invasive is the firmer establishing of such divisions in the mass media,
especially in the press and broadcasting; and in their hirelings in advertising and public relations. These changes are taking place, have come
upon us without our greatly noticing; or wishing to notice; they might
have been expected to rock the social boat. Not so; not yet.

The paradox seems to be: that working-class people —or, yes if you at last insist, what we used to call working-class people—have begun to rid themselves of that *deference* which was thought to help sustain the divisions. To that extent today's old-style snobs are walking on the water, or on air. Most working-class people have, to change the image, pulled the rug (or the red carpet) from under their feet. Levelling, assisted by the mass media and not always of an attractive kind, has rapidly taken over; and most working-class people have noticed and appeared to have accepted and acted on that; but have not yet at all taken its true measure.

One can fairly stress again that traditional working-class manners—customs at home and outside, forms of courtesy, politenesses—can be just as complex and sensitive as those of the middle class. That always needs saying during these discussions.

A trickier field is vulgarity, especially in speech. We all know that in some parts of working-class life, today as earlier, vulgar speech is everyday speech. Some workmen still cannot utter a sentence, or a clause, without lacing it with 'fuckings'. We are back with the stratifying within the working-class itself. Most did not and do not talk like that, at home or in the street. Really aspiring working-class people usually pinned and pin their aspirations on the arrival at gentility in speech and manners. One middle-aged lady, working-class but aspiring, asked a relative of ours if she was breast-feeding her first child. On being told that this was so, she added in a slightly deflated and deflating voice: 'Some people think it's not *quite nice* nowadays'.

It is easy to mock the gentility of 'toilet' or 'must go to the bathroom', and furry covers for the 'loo' (that current permitted word among the liberated), or crochetted what-nots. It is easy to point with moderate pleasure at the fact that in some ways working-class and upper-class people share the use of vulgarities in speech, if not actual idioms. The usages could hardly be the same; one comes from long connections with the land, and from the extreme social confidence that inherited rank can give; the other is the lazy coarseness of the bottom part of the urbanised working class, the adoption there of another of those local rites of passage.

Attitudes to the intellect, ideas, thought were, as we noted, for historic reasons not much available to working-class people and often slightly feared or drawn back from, but also in some ways respected. It is a growing characteristic of mass communications today—in the press, magazines and much broadcasting—that they show no respect at all for the 'life of the mind' (a good and essential phrase), but dismiss such things as elitist and not for people 'such as us'; not that 'we' now think ourselves inferior, but quite the opposite; we are members of the overwhelming majority who are going the way the world is going. This is the dead centre of popular and unassailable taste. Chat-show hosts and hostesses display it daily, television 'personalities' are pleased to indicate that they have no tastes which in any way differ from those of their mass audiences, and certainly none which might seem 'better' than those of the audiences. The broadsheet newspapers often fall backwards into those postures. Such words, words of evaluation, have fallen out of the populist lexicon. Broadcasting interviewers see themselves as 'the voice of the common man', which is a reductive myth; their 'common man' is all too often an invented vulgarian.

Even the BBC's news editors take over every fresh solecism as though it was a new, true, linguistic trope, not to be questioned. In one sense such a decline may seem too trivial to matter; in another sense it is an example of sloppy, tritely fashionable language and so of similar thought. Lord Reith would rightly and contemptuously have rejected it.

It has also begun to seem, at the turn into the new century, that a racism which has long been widespread but was for most people usually held just under the articulate surface, is rising again. This is particularly worrying since we had at last begun to feel able to say that in some cities (Leicester is often cited) a working, admirable assimilation had begun to form. Nowadays, racist opinions are being more openly expressed in word and deed than they were in the preceding few decades, the decades which allowed Parliament to pass a civilised Act against racism. If that Act (and the one against capital punishment) were not already on the statute books but were proposed today, it is not certain that either would be passed. Certainly some of the Press and those not only among the tabloids, would do their best to drive out any such bills. Just below the surface too many of our people remain uncivilised; as seen in the baying crowds outside the homes of suspected pedophiles, or in those hammering on the sides of police vans as a suspected criminal is taken to court; the editorials in some of the press stoke these fires. Against such exhibitions, one of the most popular of all adages among many of the old working class—'It takes all sorts to make a world'—begins to sound not so much like a comfortable accommodating as a horrible recognition of the awful.

Add the deep-grained brutality still practised in some prisons, the increasingly violent behaviour in cities and small towns, especially at weekends, the burgeoning 'reality' (a euphemism for 'crudely exhibitionist and exposing') programmes on television, the support given to such things and many another like them in the press on the grounds of 'democratic choice' (and the denunciation of anyone who dares criticise them). In the face of all these things one is bound to wonder just where we are heading; not to a more 'civil' society, that seems plain.

Against all this, religious belief—except for some odd alternative prescriptions—is bound to be having a very hard time. Roman Catholic rule is still tight but will gradually go the same way; it is 'undemocratic', though sometimes in a defensible sense. Religion is dying; we must all look out for ourselves; and protect ourselves from fake distractions, beginning with rejecting the worship of consumerism and false togetherness. It is inescapably a complex fate to live in a modern capitalist 'democracy'; but if you listen to all the popular voices and ignore any others the complexity can be ignored. We have to find our own moral guidelines, without benefit of formal belief or mass persuasion.

That second pillar of traditional Englishness, the Monarchy, will go also, but more slowly since it has a remarkable capacity to reinvent itself or to be reinvented; as mid-middle class. Or perhaps eventually even as part of the respectable lower-middle? That would be going too far; dissolution would be preferred; but is a long way off. The strongly elastic swinging back against the Monarchy, after its failure to recognise the popular mood on Princess Diana's death, and the Queen's subsequent reversal, illustrate that. All those apocalyptic articles defining the original failure as the beginning of the end of the Monarchy were misplaced or at best wildly premature.

That death also brought out more contradictory attitudes to the Monarchy and myths about 'the popular mind' than had been exhibited for many decades. Such as that about our cherished English 'stiff upper lip' and dislike of emotional display. For weeks our collective life was similar to, let us say, what we like to think of as the operatically self-exposing Southern Italians. The mixture of being 'a Royal', having most acceptably good looks, an open-hearted attention to some good and often dangerous causes, a pitiably bad choice in men, a disastrous and cruelly arranged marriage, the air of a wounded and not very bright bird (as she readily admitted), the inevitable neurotic illnesses—how many more chords was it possible to pluck at the same time to excite what was then revealed as the thoroughly sentimental English soul?

The most astonishing evidence of all as to the staying-power of the Monarchy was the audio-tape revelation that the heir to the throne talked to his mistress about wishing to be a sanitary-towel within her body. There's aristocratic plain-speaking with knobs on. That, even more than the overwhelming emotion shown on Princess Diana's death, opened a new page in the revelation of the astonishing English capacity to hang on to its Royals. It would have shocked our Hunslet house and our neighbours to their roots, 'to the core'. I would have mistakenly assumed that it would shock nowadays the respectable working class and the lower middle class, at the least.

On the contrary it seemed to 'sink without trace', so that one was left wondering whether there was anything at all in the behaviour of the Royal family which most of us would not accept. Becoming Roman Catholics? The heir to the throne proposing to marry a Jewess? Or 'coming out' as a homosexual? In comparison, marrying today's equivalent of Mrs. Simpson would seem easy.

Like our addiction to the Monarchy, our attachment to superstition survives in many forms and at most levels of society. Even if they have discarded religious belief, many feel a need to cling to some element of mystery in life. That clearly has a stronger hold than we are willing to admit. Has it strengthened as religious belief has waned? It would be unpleasant to think so. Officially consigned to the wings in an era of religious beliefs it has now stepped forward, though rather unconvincingly so far. It is really 'not up to' that role even though it chimes in with some of the contradictions of today's prevailing culture, being technocratic, incorrigibly worldly but also other-worldly in its homage to crackpot convictions. When will it be found out if at all; if ever?

Perhaps, aided by the most popular voices, those of the 'opinion-formers' with elastic-sided principles and with the season's celebrities bringing up the rear, we will eventually accept virtually anything. If they are challenged, say on radio or television, by someone who is prepared to try to make the case for principled and if necessary solitary commitment, those opinion formers already show themselves entirely unable to meet the argument, so encased are they in their compliant, echoing-back, media world. In the light of such major secular changes, the emergence of those two divisions noted earlier, with their separated—dumbed-down and meritocratic—approaches, was simply predictable. In such a climate, a debate about major do-mestic issues--the needs of the public service in all its forms and the limitations of privatisation, as illustrated especially in the railway and Tube systems, the NHS and Broadcasting—is hobbled from the start; as is any more demanding argument, one about, say, freedom of speech and censorship. Instead, triviality wins.

A BBC television series on past years with the general title *I Love...*; as in *I Love 1975* might have been assumed to have a wide net of important and interesting events. That particular year in-cluded the launch of the unmanned spacecraft *Viking* heading for Mars, more than one Nobel Prize for Britain, the Watergate trials, a London underground crash that killed forty-one and injured ninety, British inflation at 25 percent, several huge aircraft disasters, the Helsinki Conference on Security and Cooperation, the death of Franco, several new works by authors and other artists of repute. The programme was entirely about sport, pop music, and block-buster films; a completely low-level focus no doubt felt entirely suitable for and reflecting the tastes of the assumed audience of 'I's' in the title. *I Love My 1975* would have been a more honest, and revealing, label.

The Emerging Idioms of Relativism

So, since relativism is the prevailing attitude, and expresses itself in populism, head-counting, massing, anti-individualism in tastes and opinions, and thus in the end facelessness, all this has begun to show itself in new idioms, or, more likely, sound-bites. Yet these are early days and the linguistic changes so large and rapid that they need much more attention than would be relevant here. I hope to give them that in a *Brief Guide to the Mass Media in a Mass Society.*

The Booker Prize for Literature in 2001 was not awarded to a writer whom much public opinion had seemed to favour. At a press conference a journalist asked why therefore that writer had not won. A member of the committee gave an answer unusual in its direct-ness and firmness, to the effect that: 'This prize is not meant to be a reflection of public taste. It is a prize for literary quality'. That dis-tinction would puzzle not only the journalist but many another; again, no common ground for judgment.

The question inhabits the same mental universe as that idiom used repeatedly in discussions, the favoured idiom for the levelling impulse: 'There ought to be a level playing-field', as though life is a football game rather than an experience we have to live through, in which few playing-fields—few gifts, few talents—are, in fact, level.

At the bottom of the acceptance of relativism as the only belief is, paradoxically, a belief that there is no such thing as belief or conviction. That can do much to remove guilt or even the feeling of being somehow lost, since relativism provides a Dead Sea of common feeling in which we float, all warm and supported. The motto used to promote the soap-opera *East Enders*, repeatedly shown on television, hammers away with: 'Everyone's talking about it'. 'So what?'— is the only self-respecting response.

In such a world one phrase, which has been at hand for centuries, acquires new popularity: 'Well, if I don't do it, someone else will' (to excuse some wrong-doing, small or large). Self-justifying emptiness taking refuge in the presumed crowd of similar others.

Inevitably, mass-populism breeds its own counter-bodies, assertions of types of individuality, of insistent self-regard, solitary pugnacity, narcissism. On television, in between all the mass-mush, 'reality' programmes and increasingly hard-nosed quiz-shows proliferate, in which individuals fight to get their heads above those of the crowd, by which the rest are at best abashed, at worst humiliated. This is one source of the urge to win on the Lottery: to get out of the ruck. Consider in this perspective also programmes such as *Big Brother, Castaway, Who Wants to be a Millionaire?* And, most striking of all, *Dog Eat Dog* and *The Weakest Link*. There are several others; and we are, of course, promised a succession of even 'better' such inventions.

The word 'community' is still warmly over-used and misused. But look at the new type of insurance. The old style used to admit those of most ages; the facts that you were getting on a bit, or your house was not fairly new, was not determining. Exclude those and premiums are kept down for the young, in post-war houses. The old in their older houses can fend for themselves. Not much 'sharing', community, spirit there.

A Labour Party manifesto of 1997 had a slogan advising 'you' to vote for them: 'Because you deserve better'. Again, not much communal socialist principle there. It has been surpassed by the 'You owe it to yourself' range as in the supermarket tag on its 'better' products: 'Be good to yourself'. Even that is outclassed by the purely narcissistic claim that 'you' should use a certain perfume: 'because I'm worth it'. 'Because you're worth it' sounds out of date, but expresses at least some sense of affection for another. 'Because I'm worth it' is self-enclosed, talking to itself, wrapped in total egotism.

It promises not to be the last of its kind; it suggests a sort of air-hole out of mass-populism but also lives comfortably within it, a minor reverse reflection not a revolt; an early example of the new breed of socially compatible sound-bites. It already has cousins in the same field and also, predictably, in drink and car advertisements.

If only more politicians, more broadcasters, more journalists, more citizens would look much more closely at what has been no more than sketched in these last few pages, we might have a better, a more 'decent' democratic future. There are, so far, not many encouraging signs.

Index